HENRY THOREAU

AMERICAN REBEL

HENRY THOREAU

AMERICAN REBEL

T. MORRIS LONGSTRETH

Illustrated with photographs by Edwin Way Teale

New York

DODD, MEAD & COMPANY

Printed in the United States of America
by The Haddon Craftsmen, Inc., Scranton, Penna.

To Margaret Whitney Byerly

Acknowledgments

THE writers and other friends who have helped me to know Henry Thoreau during the past sixty-some years are literally too numerous to mention.

My seven years' residence in Henry's own Concord brought me in touch with all phases of his existence. The home of Allen and Aletta French was the chief meeting place of the Sunday evening Thoreau Reading Circle. I walked to Walden with Townsend Scudder in winter, and in summer with some of the country's leading Thoreauvians: Dr. Raymond Adams, Edwin Way Teale, Walter Harding, and many others. Henry Seidel Canby told me much about our common hero. The Concord Antiquarian Society Thoreau room made Henry visible through his flute and other properties that had surrounded him at Walden.

But most of these "acknowledgments" must go to the man's own writings. It's a little like his own admonition, "When you travel to the Celestial City, carry no letter of introduction. When you knock, ask to see God,—none of the servants."

Foreword

MOST of our inventions extend our own selves. The phone gives our voices mileage, television expands our sight, and the coming space capsule will do for our curiosity outward what the X ray does inward. Our machines equip us for a richer and more glorious life—if we have the glory in us first.

Books do more than these mechanisms; they help supply the glory. They have made available the wisdom of the race in the Bible and the great histories. They have given us life-long friends in Shakespeare's plays and Dickens' novels and Mark Twain's stories. Anyone who has met Mr. Pickwick or Huck Finn or the Pooh can never be entirely lonely. They are permanent friends.

Best of all, books give us their creators, the wise and great and funny and lasting people who saw deeper into human beings and farther into spiritual greatness than most of us. Anybody who can read soon starts acquiring friends of this sort, and quite by accident I fell in step with Henry Thoreau when I was thirteen. I was as wild-feeling as he, as crazy about weather and the woods and rivers. I liked to laugh just as much. This happened in 1899, and we are better friends than ever today.

This is because I wanted to be I, and he wanted to be completely himself. It is because I wanted more life, and his suggestions as to how to get it were simpler, more practical and more exciting than any I heard elsewhere. It is because I wanted to be rich and lazy, to live in the country and have everything the city offered, to stay young however old I had to be, to enjoy every moment in spite of everything. The evening I first looked into Thoreau's Journals in the Westtown School library, was one of the great beginning moments of my whole existence. And I am still turning to them for pleasure and laughs, for aspects of nature I have overlooked, for good practical common sense, and, above all, for my friend Henry Thoreau. "The bluebird carries the sky on his back," he said, and Henry Thoreau carries the fire of life in his sentences. The more of them you have made your own, the richer and wiser you will be.

Westtown, Pennsylvania   T. M. L.

Contents

Foreword   ix

1 Henry in Rebellion   1

2 Henry's Concord   19

3 College Boy   43

4 A New Thing in Schools   57

5 The River Trip with John   74

6 A Love, a Death, and a Decision   92

7 The New York Intermission   122

8 A Fresh Start   129

9 Trial by Self-Reliance   139

10 Henry vs. the Times   173

11 The Summing-Up   187

Bibliography   199

Index   201

Illustrations

Following page 112

Bronze bust of Thoreau by Malvina Hoffman
Old Indian trail, Walden
Walden Pond, from the air
Thoreau's hut at Walden—and map
Thoreau's cane, inkstand and glass
Warbler's nest, piece of hut-timber, library record book
Thoreau's grave
Walden Pond

HENRY THOREAU

AMERICAN REBEL

ONE

Henry in Rebellion

THE stocky, sun-tanned boy leaned out an upper window of his home in Concord, Massachusetts, watching the martins impatiently.

Although he was not quite fifteen, he had trained himself to observe his country world accurately, in the manner of the Indians. It thrilled him that they had chosen Concord's woods and riverbanks as their gathering places. He had learned to walk with Indian alertness and use his eyes as scouts, in their fashion.

His skill in seeing had come slowly, but now he had it. With his brother John's help, Henry Thoreau had grown able to identify the various winged individuals which most people lumped together as "birds." These martins fascinated him. He had not noticed before that they flew in arcs and curves, like the lines in his geometry book. They wove their airy patterns so rapidly that no print was left on his memory. Blackbirds he could follow: they wheeled like the soldiers he had watched on Boston Common. Hawks soared, buzzards glided, flickers undulated as if riding billows of air, sparrows flitted, and crows plodded like tired farmhands coming home from work. But martins . . .

Henry glanced again at the sun—stuck in the same place. It seemed dead set against setting. (The pun tickled him; he must remember to tease his sister Helen with it.) But his impatience remained. His otherwise sensible family bade him stay indoors until its disc slid below the horizon. Such was the Sabbath custom in this year of the Lord, 1832, and kept with Puritanical strictness in New England. In Concord, the Reverend Ezra Ripley saw to it that his flock obeyed. Each year, active Henry was more irked by this imprisonment. His Aunt Maria declared that he was outdoors-mad and would never be civilized.

The boy's alert ears caught the sound of a muffled booming downstairs. Uncle Charles must have waked up. Uncle Charles Dunbar, the wild brother of Henry's mother, often embarrassed the Thoreaus. Henry admired him defiantly; but, according to Aunt Maria, the young firebrand liked all the wrong people, such as One-eyed Goodwin, and George Melvin, and other riffraff.

Henry chuckled as the bellowing grew louder. Uncle Charles's voice could be heard across Concord on a still day. Once he had relayed a message from the shore to a vessel at sea by hollering across the water. Fortunately, Uncle Charles napped most of the time when he came to call.

Abruptly, the door flew open and the big man strode in. "Why, you young rebel!" he roared at Henry. "They tell me you don't like being caged up till sundown. That's the Huguenot in you."

"What's a Huguenot?" Henry demanded.

"What's a Huguenot?" Uncle Charles mimicked. "For grief's sake! Don't they teach you about your kin? When

Madame Philippe Thoreau was forbidden to worship in France according to her conscience, she up and took the Thoreau family to the Island of Jersey, along with a lot of other Huguenots. There's the spunk I like to see." He leaned closer to Henry. "Keep a-kicking against their silly old laws, boy—for the old woman's sake. All the world loves a rebel—about a hundred years later." Uncle Charles chuckled and poked Henry playfully in the ribs.

"When I heard you wanted out in God's outdoors, I reminded the company downstairs that you came by your rebel nature honestly and I hoped you'd slide out the window. Good grief! You might suppose I'd whistled for Satan himself."

Henry could imagine the long face his Aunt Maria had drawn, and his own frown relaxed. "George Melvin thinks it's funny. He asks why a houseful of cheerful people should spend Sunday the way Old Testament folks thought proper three thousand years ago. He says the Mill Dam merchants talk progress all week and then get stuck back in the year 1000 B.C. on Sundays."

"Good for George!" roared Uncle Charles. "He's a thinker. Has he caught any more pa'tridges singlehanded? Now there's a man I'd like to wrassle. I could bust him, though."

Henry dared to reveal more of his rebellious ideas to this sympathetic friend. "It doesn't make *me* more religious to be jailed so—no games, no book that isn't preachy, the music box locked, and no talk that would not be thought uplifting."

"Like ours now!" Uncle Charles guffawed so heartily that the ceiling appeared in danger.

The door opened timidly, and Henry's younger sister,

3

Sophia, asked if she might come in. She was a gentle girl, rather homely, but full of affection, especially for Henry. Standing close by her brother, she looked straight at Uncle Charles and said bravely, "I . . . I don't believe it about the houses."

"Now what've I said wrong?" the big man demanded.

"You told Mother we were nomads, picking up and moving from one house to another, like squirrels. You said we must have lived in fifteen houses. You said we were no better than gypsies and ought to grow shelters on our backs like turtles."

At this moment, Henry's older brother, John, entered the room. At eighteen, he was a good-looking young man, considerably taller than the boy, pleasanter to look at, with less of a nose and more of a chin. By nature he was everything that Henry sometimes would have liked to be: cheerful with everybody, fond of girls, and able to make any girl he liked devoted to him. Ignoring the others, John said to Henry, "I can't go on the river this evening. I'm sorry. I told Ed Hoar I'd come over."

Sophia giggled and said to Henry, "As if it was *Ed* he's going to see!"

Henry felt let down. He had counted on the boat ride with John. He silently loved his older brother with all his nature and had looked up to him since babyhood. Now he could say nothing, and John vanished.

Sophia returned to the charge and said to Uncle Charles, "I don't believe we've lived in *ten* houses, so there!"

Henry interrupted with "*I've* lived in eight already, Sophy. Uncle Charles is right; we'd do better as turtles, and keep to one swamp. I'd like that."

4

"You *would!*" But Sophia giggled again. "At least the mosquitoes wouldn't bite us. I doubt you can name all eight houses."

"Certainly I can. There was Grandma Minott's house on Virginia Road here, where I was born. Then the Red House, on Lexington Road . . ."

"A double house," Uncle Charles put in. "I lived in t'other side and had to listen to your mother night and day. The plaguy walls were made of tissue paper, it seemed like."

"Then Father took the store in Chelmsford," Henry went on, as if Uncle Charles had not interrupted. "Then Boston."

"Another store. Corner of Pope and Pinckney Streets," Uncle Charles added.

"Then Concord again," Henry resumed. "In the Brick House on Main Street and Walden Road, and next the Davis House, by the Hoar place, and now here in the Shattuck House."

"For five whole years already!" jeered Uncle Charles. "You're slowin' down. Five years! That's palsy! That's paralysis!"

Henry glanced out the window and gave a whoop. The sun was halfway below the horizon. He headed for the door.

"Where are you going?" Sophia called. But Henry was out of sight; they could hear him taking three steps at a time down the staircase.

"There's a boy after my own heart," Uncle Charles said. "When John leaves the room, it's like putting out a light. But Henry's my bet. He's going to *be* somebody. He won't trail around, usual Thoreau-fashion. Not Henry."

Sophia loved her uncle for that praise. She was devoted to Henry, but her affectionate nature cherished all the family

5

and her uncle's mild derision worried her. "Uncle Charles," she began hesitantly, "why did Father trail around so?"

"You really want to know?" Cynthia Thoreau's brother, who was part comedian, part show-off strong man, part actor, looked into the puzzled blue eyes of the thirteen-year-old girl and wondered what to tell her. "Your father is too good, sweetheart. He'd sooner lose a hand than do anybody in trade. He's too soft-natured to collect money owed him. He's too contented to be ambitious and make money. He has tried teaching and storekeeping and farming and run into a lot of hard luck. But I've noticed that if you stay yourself and don't try to be somebody else, bad luck gets tired and goes away, and good luck comes, and now your father's found out what he really can do well."

"You mean making pencils?"

"Just that, Sophia." She had rarely seen her boisterous Uncle Charles so serious. "Like all he-Thoreaus, your father is able with his hands. Even head-in-air Henry can make anything he pleases. Your father is so honest that he couldn't make a bad pencil, let alone sell one. He's turned the corner, I warrant. And now I've got to turn one—on the road home. Give your noisy old uncle a kiss, little homebody, and paint my picture someday, will you?"

Sophia braced herself for the vigorous kiss and blushed at this request for a portrait. She loved to do water colors of flowers, but they looked so *feeble* beside real flowers. She loved the flowers better herself, almost better than people, except Henry. She would do anything for Henry—and he didn't care a mite. . . . Perhaps he really did, only he wouldn't show it.

She followed her uncle downstairs and decided to go out

now and pick a bouquet for Aunt Jane to take home with
her. It was considered a sin to pick flowers on the Sabbath,
but maybe God didn't agree with the Reverend Ezra Ripley
on that. He *couldn't*. That was what Henry said, anyway,
and Henry thought a lot about such things.

Henry, freed at last from those four walls and the restric-
tions of "sanctity," headed full stride for the river, half a mile
away. Thanks to his persistent search into Indian ways, he
had read how to plant each foot straight, how to stretch the
reach of each leg. So, although his legs were short, he covered
the ground rapidly, evenly, and without tiring.

On the bank of the quiet river he surprised a large snap-
ping turtle and laughed at its ungainly movements. It looked
like a man trying to walk by sticking his legs and arms out of
the windows.

The square-headed boat was clumsy and heavy. It required a strong shoulder and sound footing to shove it into
the water. He and John must make another, if he could
stop his brother from visiting the Hoar girls long enough.
Since this boat was impossible to upset, and so had saved his
mother anxiety, it had helped him procure his freedom. It did
well enough as a movable home. Once on the river, he was
safe from capture and from other people's demands. That
was the thing, to be free!

Henry pushed the boat out upon the placid river whither
the shadows were heading, too. Fortunately, July twilights
were long. He gazed up into the vast serenity of sky and was
thankful that the world was not roofed. The birds had perpetual freedom up there.

7

Henry liked to stalk a thought the way an Indian stalked a deer. A thought was like an unexplored trail. It was fun to find out where it led. And now he let the boat glide with the hardly noticeable current while he scanned the sky and savored his freedom. He valued this feeling of utter freedom above everything. Why didn't other people enjoy it more? His father was content to be shut into the pencil shop all day long. The storekeepers on the Mill Dam were caged up like so many starlings, yet they didn't complain. How could live men become like that?

No thought answered him and he fitted the oars between the upright pegs and began to row gently, almost noiselessly, except for the drip of water from the oar blades. Even so, he startled a heron into the air. He was amused by the awkwardness of its flight—two wide, undulating wings pinned together, and it looked as if its body and neck had been left behind on the bank.

Presently Henry reached one of the grassy places where the Indians had pitched their wigwams on the bank of the stream. He pretended that the dusk concealed the little settlement. He thought of the men spearing fish in the river. He and John had copied them. While John propelled the boat, he had stood in the bow with a torch in one hand and his homemade harpoon in the other. Henry was sad at being born too late for the Indian life. Of course it was safer now. No painted brave was likely to leap out from behind a bush and scalp him. But no boy he knew would have let the chance of a scalping keep him from being a hunter when these woods were full of game.

The next best thing, Henry thought, would have been to

be one of the earliest pioneers, to have come with Simon Willard and Peter Bulkeley to pick a site for a frontier settlement. No wonder the Musketaquid region had delighted them. Its seven natural ponds, its two rivers and countless streams offered fish and beaver. And the Indians' cornfields showed the soil's richness.

But how unwary of white men the Indians were! Henry thought with some indignation. Right there in Concord Square, where his aunts lived, the whites had set about taking over the land from its red-skinned owners—for some beads and calico. Simon Willard was reckoned a shrewd trader because he had pointed to the four quarters of the world and declared he had purchased all the land within three miles of the great buttonwood tree they were standing under—east, west, north, and south.

It made Henry hot to think about it. If only he had been there, he would have sought out the Indian chief and have tried to make him understand he was being cheated. The Indians, comprehending nothing, looked at the two dollars' worth of trinkets and consented. Only last spring, in his history class at Concord Academy, Henry had declaimed against this theft and stated that they all were living on stolen property. And how everybody had howled at him for sticking up for the savages! But a few laughs didn't bother Henry; he was sure he was right.

Well, it was *his* territory now, without anyone being cheated. He had got it back from the whites without their knowing. He did not even need a bagful of beads. It gave him a pleasant rascally feeling to own all he could see without having to barter anything except his time and eyesight and a little exertion. The slow-flowing river was his Main Street; nor did he have to pay those taxes that people talked so much about at Town Meeting. He harvested fish from the river free of cost. The Hosmers and Buttricks, the Meriams and Flints, and all the other families raised blueberries for him at the expense of a little perspiration on his part.

Henry rowed more quickly now under the stimulus of his happy thoughts. He owed most to his own eyes. Eyes were gatherers of nuts and arrowheads, of hawks and owls, of turtles and muskrats, of clouds and colors and every change of color, charge-free. Thanks to them, he often picked up an idea worth keeping. His eyes and his mind worked together, like his two hands. Only yesterday, he had been looking at the big white pine on Revolutionary Ridge and realized that it stood there like an Indian—untamed, with a strange wildness about it. Why had that never occurred to him before? Because he hadn't been thinking distinctly about what he was looking at. The thought came less from what you looked at than from what you *saw*. He must remember that and train himself to see past the thing he was looking at to the thought in its shadow.

Night was nearing. He could hardly peer any distance into the woods. But night was as good as day for his purposes, for enjoying. Night was the better time to hear—to explore with your ears. As he thought of this, he heard sounds. Someone was chopping and Henry laughed quietly, for he remembered what his Aunt Maria said on similar occasions, "Henry, have you forgotten what day this is?"

Someone was forgetting—on purpose, Henry thought with amusement, and he guessed it was One-eyed Goodwin. That hardy bachelor was Concord's head rascal. The good people of Concord were apt at calling names if they didn't like the way you lived. Henry didn't much mind name-calling and he doubted that Goodwin minded either—he was having too good a time living his way. Nor could he be a very bad man, Henry considered; he was so cheery. Henry had already noticed that joy and badness seldom went hand in hand.

He tugged at the oars, the boat rounded a bend, and he made out a rowboat pulled up beside the bank. By its load—some driftwood, a bucket, a gun leaning against its side—Henry knew that the lawless pirate (in Aunt Maria's estimation) was seeking booty on Deacon Henslow's land. The happy outlaw made no mystery of the way he got his living. He lifted it where he found it—fish from the river, game birds from the marshes, partridges from the woods, anybody's woods, and firewood from stranded flood debris or closer home. Most of the owners overlooked Goodwin's thefts, because he took only what would not be used, such as this stump which Henry reached as the lawless fellow finished chopping.

Goodwin greeted Henry easily and said, "Got a message for you from Minott. He wants you to come see him in the morning."

"What's he want?"

"Didn't say."

The patch over Goodwin's left eye looked more buccaneerish than ever in the gloom. Henry helped carry some of the wood to the boat and said, "You didn't stay in the house till sundown, if you chopped all this today."

"Me? Why should I?" Goodwin chuckled. "I like that

rule. It's a good rule, shutting everybody up. Then nobody's out to warn me off his land. I ain't seen a soul but Perch Hosmer out fur pickerel. He must know the taste of 'em by now."

"How did he get named Perch?"

"Don't you know? Why, he used ter help draw the seine back of Jones's house. One time he hauled in without getting a single shad. He held up a little perch in sport above his face, to show what he'd netted. The perch wiggled just then and dropped right down Hosmer's throat, head foremost. It nigh suffocated him. Only after a lot of back pounding and belly punching was the perch knocked out—or most probably forced down. Anyways, Hosmer was in a worse fix than a fish hawk, and they call him Perch ever since."

Henry was enjoying himself. This was the kind of harvesting that he liked—gathering in the life that was really lived from the people who lived it and talked little. George Minott was that kind—he must remember to visit George early.

Henry left Goodwin reluctantly, but he was aware that his mother would worry if he stayed out too long. It was almost night now up there in the birds' ocean. He had never thought of it as the birds' ocean before, where the bathers swam with their wings. Were there really other shores to that ocean? Other worlds? He stopped rowing and lay back against a thwart. He liked to drift at times. That was when ideas floated to you. His cat Min caught her mice by sitting still. But even without mice in mind, she loved to bask in the sun. Perhaps that was why cats were so wise. They weren't busybodies. They didn't "improve their time," as Henry was so repeatedly instructed to do; they lived it. He wished Min could talk, but no, it was better that she didn't. She might start instructing him, too.

Tomorrow he would be busy enough, Henry thought with a mental shrug. He would be striving to accomplish something in a fluster of activity. His mother would be preserving the blackberries that he would pick. His father would be making more pencils in a fog of dust, with John helping him. Helen would be sewing on her quilt and Sophia cleaning the lamps and silver after the two had made the beds.

Henry chuckled aloud at that word *made*. He pictured his all-but-helpless sisters with saws, hammers, chisels, boards, wooden pegs, lathe-turned legs, and whipcord *making* new beds every morning. Seeing that neither of them could drive a nail straight, they would be smart girls to have one bed made by suppertime. Lucky they didn't have to *make* the sheets and blankets too, and do a thorough job of it!

So much for a word. Henry found he liked words. They were good playthings, especially puns, which everybody pretended to be outraged by. Here Henry's musing was interrupted by a signal from his feet. He bent forward. Yes, the boat was leaking. Well, Goodwin declared that when he went fishing it was better for the boat to leak a little. His brother John would not agree. John liked everything just right.

Henry reached the landing place, dragged the heavy boat up, then, with a strong lift, turned it over, and suddenly felt good. He could do it alone. He was growing strong, really strong. What was more, he could fix the leaky seam without John's help. Spruce gum, melted, would be the thing, and then some lead paint. He'd do the painting, too.

13

As he headed home, he hoped that John would have had enough of the Hoar girls and be back, too. But anyway the river had saved Sunday for him. He would tell no one that. John would understand, but nobody else. It would be his secret.

When Uncle Charles and Sophia had followed the fleeing Henry downstairs, they found the usual gathering of family and aunts in the sitting room:

John senior, quiet, rather ungainly in his Sunday suit, and looking a little lost without tools or newspaper;

Cynthia Dunbar Thoreau, half a head taller than her husband, a born manager, and so interested in everybody that she must report their every doing, often caustically, if displeased;

Helen Thoreau, oldest of the four children, and teaching music now;

Maria Thoreau, Father John's sister, tending to be masterful and overly abundant in opinion;

Jane, Maria's sister, so often rebuked by Maria that she seemed quiet almost to lifelessness.

Although the ladies were not sorry to see him back, Uncle Charles did not tarry. The atmosphere was too domestic to suit his swaggering nature, and he was perpetually running afoul of the bustling, intelligent, vigorous Cynthia. But Sophia sat down on the horsehair-covered chair by her father and listened to her Aunt Maria's strictures on Henry's un-Sabbathlike haste.

Helen looked in annoyance at her aunt and said, "When

Dr. Ripley spoke of heaven this morning, he made it sound far away. But for Henry it begins at the back door."

"And is that an advantage?" Maria retorted severely. "I never saw such a boy. He can't be like anybody else."

"He would consider that a compliment," Cynthia observed quickly.

Father John, ever eager to maintain harmony, interposed, "Henry could do worse than take to the woods, Sister. He is careful not to waste his time there. John is compiling a list of the Massachusetts birds, and Henry is helping by watching out for rare species."

Cynthia spoke up. "John and I took the children into the woods as soon as they could fare there, Maria. We're happy that they share our love of nature. So reproach us instead of the boy, if you please."

"I was intending no reproach," Aunt Maria countered. "I have learned how useless that is. But it is time that Henry should discover more civilized interests than snakes swallowing toads. He started to tell me about *that* and I had to beg him to desist! Presumably he is preparing for Harvard and must consider something more suitable than reptiles and the lore of that dreadful man with a patch over his eye."

"Goodwin," Helen supplied the name.

"That's the fellow. A disgrace to the neighborhood." Maria turned to her brother, "I do think, John, that you should advocate more refined company for your son."

Cynthia was nettled. "You talk as if Henry were on the brink of perdition, Maria, simply because he enjoys the company of these men who live so close to nature. They supply a second education. . . ."

15

"I can believe that," Maria interrupted crisply.

"I have yet to hear an unsavory word from Henry's mouth, Sister," John Thoreau said gravely.

"And I thank Heaven that Phineas Allen hasn't been able to whip curiosity out of him!" Cynthia exclaimed warmly. "From what I hear, Phineas thrashes much too readily."

"Henry doesn't scare," Sophia put in gently.

"He never cried as a baby," Aunt Jane contributed. "When Dr. Ripley baptized him, and the water drops fell on his face, he didn't even whimper, as most babies do. Henry just stared at Dr. Ripley as if daring him to do it again, and never a squeal."

"Henry never has learned when he should be scared," Cynthia said. "The moment he could toddle, he'd hold out his hand to any mongrel coming down the street. I remember the time when I tried to milk our brindle cow, the one that kicked so, and Henry, afraid of naught as usual, got the breath kicked out of him. *I* was the scared one."

Helen who had heard these stories too often, changed the subject abruptly. "Is it decided that Henry is to go to Harvard, Mamma?"

"That is our intention, certainly. John would have gone if we could have afforded to send him."

"Oh, I'm so glad!" Sophia exclaimed. "Henry loves books as much as he loves outdoors. What vexes him is that most people don't *really* love either."

"I think Henry is rather young to set himself up as a judge," Aunt Maria said tartly. "He is overready with his opinions of people!"

"And where did he get that aptitude?" Cynthia asked.

It was time for Father John to temper the talk again and he said, "Henry will be fifteen on the twelfth of this month. . . ."

The girls and Cynthia laughed aloud at this reminder—as if they hadn't been preparing for Henry's birthday for weeks. Helen said, "Henry should have been born on the Fourth of July, instead of the twelfth, he's so independent."

"Then he'd probably think the firecrackers were for him!" Aunt Maria put in. "I don't know where he gets his conceit from, John. Certainly not from you." Then she looked at Cynthia as if to say, "Of course, he has only one other parent."

"Please let me finish," her brother urged gently. "I believe Harvard provides scholarships for worthy candidates."

"Yes. I inquired," Cynthia said. "Phineas Allen suggests that Henry mention Dr. Ripley, Mr. Hoar, and Mr. Emerson as references. I'm told that Henry's board, at a commons table, costs $1.35 a week. We could manage that if I take an extra boarder. His wardrobe . . ."

The girls' laughter started again. "Oh, Mamma!" Sophia exclaimed. "*Wardrobe?* When Henry has only one coat?"

At this moment the door burst open and John junior entered. His brown hair was a little wind-tossed, color was high in his cheeks, and love of life shone in his eyes. Sophia thought that he had never looked handsomer. She envied the Hoar girls, although John had not confided which of the two town beauties attracted him the more. They were both charming and, alas, rather above the Thoreaus' social station in Concord.

"Has Henry gone?" John was asking his mother. And on

hearing that he had left the house, he added, "Do you know which way?"

"When did Henry ever tell?" replied Helen of the high brow.

"John," Sophia began, but she was too late—John was gone. "Oh, dear!" she sighed. "I wanted him to bring me a water lily."

"I declare, those boys should have been twins," Aunt Jane said quietly. "They're inseparable."

"Twins? Nonsense!" Aunt Maria sniffed. "They're as different as day and night. And it's Henry who is night."

"*That* is nonsense indeed!" Cynthia retorted. "Henry can be as sunny as noon. Nobody in this house laughs more."

"But such puns!" objected Helen, who was slightly pedantic. "He made a dreadful one this morning while watching the cat. He said he knew which part of the Holy Land Min would have liked best—Mouse-opotamia!"

Nobody did Henry the honor of laughing at this quip, although Sophia did supply a giggle.

"Henry verges on the sacrilegious at times," Aunt Maria observed.

"I am thankful that he has a sense of humor," Cynthia replied. "It is not granted to everyone."

John, the ever-watchful peacemaker, rose to indicate that the Sabbath bonds could be loosed and said to Cynthia, "I think we could all do with a cup of tea. I'll start the fire."

TWO

Henry's Concord

HENRY woke early the next morning and remembered the message from George Minott. Without waiting for breakfast, he ran barefoot along the dusty Boston Road, with the rising sun in his face. His Grandma Dunbar had married Jonas Minott, after Grandpa Asa's death, so George was some sort of relative. But that was not why Henry felt so much at home with this middle-aged farmer.

Minott loved his lot, his way of life. Most of the farmers Henry talked with thought of their farms as money-making machinery. They were forever grumbling because they made less money than they hoped. But George Minott lived for satisfaction, just as Henry did. He liked to take his time, as Henry stubbornly did.

The boy puffed to a walk at the bottom of Minott's rise of ground. His small, square, one-storied, unpainted house seemed fairly lodged on that south slope, as if planted there, a sturdier crop than most. Henry liked Minott's way of doing without graveled walks, flower plots, and fenced front yard. It was wilder this way. The house looked out over the road, meadow, and brook to distant woods.

Henry fancied that Minott knew more of what was going

on in Concord than most of the villagers. But it was Minott's news of woods and streams that Henry wanted, the reports on the wildlife that the Mill Dam ignored. Only last week Minott had said, "As soon as the nights cool off a bit, I can step outdoors at nine of the evening, when all is still, and I can hear the foxes barking out there on the flat behind the Lexington Road houses. That's half a mile, and yet I can sometimes hear them *whistle* through their noses."

Henry stowed that news in his memory; he must pick a still evening and hear a fox whistling through his nose. Best of all, he could trust George. He called things by the right name and said only what he believed. The boy gravitated to such a man. Henry wanted to be like him, to speak sincerely. Doing this was a kind of adventure; for people, he had found out, didn't like it always. At school, the boys sometimes jeered at him for saying what he was sure was so when it disagreed with their easy notions. He would have liked to pass on the news about foxes whistling through their noses. How they would scoff and end up by throwing his cap up into the crotch of an elm. He had better hear a fox whistling first. Then he could be *sure.*

Henry found Minott in his woodshed, which was furnished with seats for visitors—sawed-off blocks of wood, a patchwork mat on the wheelbarrow, a board on the sawhorse. A saucy pullet was perched on the farmer's shoulder, and one on his knee was letting him stroke it.

Minott said, "Good! I like to see a boy traveling with the sun. It's a sign he's in health. Now, children," and he brushed the chickens away, "I've other business than petting you. Go find a worm."

He led Henry to the barn and pointed up to a box that

HENRY'S CONCORD

served as a barn-swallow's nest. "There's five young in it," he whispered. "Now watch that opening."

Almost at once, the mother swallow darted into the barn with a moth in her beak. The gaping mouth of the nestling sitting in the little doorway accepted the meal, swallowed it in a visible gulp, and the mother was off again.

"Now they all hitch around one notch," Minott said. "See? That's so a new mouth'll be ready for the next bait."

And so it was. Henry was surprised by the promptness of the mother-bird's return. He watched the youngster in the doorway take the second morsel. Then he, too, was nudged out of place by the next in the receiving line.

"Isn't that a sight?" Minott exclaimed quietly. "This goes on as regular as beads on a string. The same young un never gets two meals in succession."

Henry had already noticed how deftly the next-in-turn shouldered the last receiver out of the way. He continued to watch, fascinated. Then a hitch occurred. The mother brought so small an insect that the young bird in the doorway felt that he was not getting his share, and so waited for the next offering. His successor nudged and bumped and made small twitters of outrage, but the obstinate one stood his ground.

"Now what?" Henry asked. Minott pointed at the mother who had just arrived with a moth of the desired size. She refused to drop it into the waiting one's mouth. Instead, she held the moth in her claws while she scolded the fledgling until it moved on. Then she fed the next in line.

"How's that? Minott asked. "They don't need to go to law about it. No, sir. They know what's what without a judge swallow and a dozen jury swallows getting paid to tell them."

"But the nestling who got the too-small bug knew what was *fair!*" Henry protested. "Don't you think he was right?"

Minott shook his head. "That's the way things come, boy, and you've got to make the best of it, like weather. The mother bird can't stop to weigh each bug. It's turn and turn about, and no unfairness intended. Now you count and watch. Maybe the mother'll bring a bigger one next time to the baby who thought he was cheated."

Henry watched without noticing any more trouble. . . . Finally, he thought that he should go home and said, "I'm glad you sent that message, George."

"I knew you'd find it worthwhile coming to see, Henry. I sized you up the first time we run into each other."

"I remember. In the woods below Fair Haven Hill. You'd just caught that partridge by the wing."

"Yes, and you believed me when I said I had. A man likes to be believed. Especially when he's telling what looks like a first-class whopper. I reckoned right then and there that I and you'd be friends."

Henry was glad inside but unable to give voice to the reason why he had believed George. Minott respected his silence and said, "I don't have to be a fortune teller to guess you haven't had breakfast yet, Henry. I can hear by the pans it's time to break our fast, as our ancestors must have kept saying until the words got stuck together."

George's interest in words was another thing that made him different from other farmers and attracted Henry to him. Minott used old English words that Henry had never heard before, but there they were in the dictionary when he looked them up.

22

Henry pumped a basinful of water to wash his hands and Mrs. Minott made him feel at home by saying, "Sit right down and begin before the porridge cools, Henry. What can we do to make you come oftener?"

"Do what they do at home," Henry said with a beginning grin. "Give me chores. I'm a pretty steady guest there."

"I don't know what chores George could spare. He's a do-it-yourself man."

Henry noticed that the food before him was all home-raised, including the oats that made the porridge, the honest cream, so rich it had trouble moving, the wheat of the bread, the butter churned by Mrs. Minott, the cherries in the pie, not to mention the eggs and milk and the sugar for the porridge from the grove of sugar maples out back.

Nothing much was said at the meal, which demanded the hungry eaters' attention, but every word spoken, Henry thought, was a reminder of its speaker's honesty. It could not occur to Mrs. Minott or her husband to pretend a feeling or a sentiment. Being with such people strengthened Henry in his own way of living. Never since he could remember had he deceived himself or another by saying he liked something that he didn't like. He could see that frankness fretted some people, but telling something less than the truth disturbed him. Why be different from what you were? If you weren't yourself, you lost some hold on yourself. A steady liar might even vanish and instead be the other person he had pretended to be. He wanted to be himself, and intended to be, and George Minott showed him, all unconsciously, how satisfactory it was to be yourself to the full.

After the meal, Minott took his gun to the bench outdoors

and began cleaning it. "You still carry a gun everywhere, Henry?" he asked.

Henry shook his head. "I've got over wishing to be thought a man," he answered with a shy smile.

"Maybe that's a sign you are one, then," Minott said gravely.

"I used to lug that gun with me all day." Henry went on. "John did, too. There's not much we wish to kill now." His blue eyes lighted up with a remembered joy. "Last Friday I was hoeing around the corn and a song sparrow perched on my shoulder."

"He knew a friend, maybe."

"It made me feel better than winning that spelling bee last spring."

Minott nodded. "Nothing like having birds and animals trust you to make you feel right."

For honesty's sake, Henry added, "He stayed only a moment."

"That's the sparrow way. You didn't expect him to nest there, did you?"

Henry chuckled. "No, but John's squirrel wants to. John brought in a baby red squirrel he found near the tree that a squall knocked over last May. He fed it milk and it grew fast. It likes best to sleep in John's hip pocket, and it's always crawling about my shirt collar, trying to get inside it with me."

"I reckon your cat'd like to hide it." Minott's sun-cured face creased in a smile.

"Min did watch, so last week John decided that the

24

squirrel had better shift for himself, and we took him to Squirrel-town."

Henry was pleased by the surprise on Minott's face. "Squirrel-town? Now where would that be? I thought I knew all the towns here abouts."

"It's over Nutville way," Henry explained gravely.

"You trying to flummox me?" Minott asked.

The boy's eyes could no longer restrain a twinkle, and he set about revealing the secret that he knew John would not mind his telling Minott. For the brothers, there were two Concords that occupied exactly the same place geographically, but the names on their maps differed almost totally. The published map of the village and township, with the roads and rivers and hills familiar to every Concordian, told these two young naturalists little of what they really wanted to know.

So Henry and John had made a map of nature's geography for practical reference and called it *Natural Concord*. John's prime interest was birds and he marked the places where certain species could oftenest be found: Blackbird Meadows, Sheldrake Center, Osprey Wood, and Hawk Mountain— which was Fair Haven Cliff on the villagers' map. Henry added Thrush Alley, back of Revolutionary Ridge.

Henry's interests included fishing and berrrying. So he located Pickerel Place, Cranberry Island, Grapeland, and Trout Corners, where Minnow Brook ran into the Assabet.

As hunters, the brothers set down Muskrat Bottoms, Fox Run, Turtle Cove, and Woodchuck Hollow. Henry's sense of humor suggested Catamount Common for the wilder reaches of the township down stream, although no catamounts had been seen in the countryside in his lifetime. Henry also entered Arrowhead Mount, Flint Cove, and Wigwam Place on their map. Since Henry was a poet at heart, as well as naturalist, wayfarer, and humorist, he felt secretly pround of the name he had given Revolutionary Ridge—Moccasin Tread Ridge.

Minott approved of this map and said, "That's the real Concord, if you ask me. But we're lucky that the other one ain't all bricked up like Boston. I don't see how a fellow can breathe there."

On his way home, Henry realized how fortunate he was to be living in a village that nature had far from relinquished. Concord's roads were richly shaded with buttonwoods, maples, and elms, and the plain houses were painted so white that they were lost in a snow storm and became one with it.

Even the village's heart, the Square, was green with grass and trees. The business block opening off it, which housed most of the shops—and gossips—retained its country past in its name, the Mill Dam. The country was always trying to get back into the village, Henry fancied, when he saw the lawns reaching to the river and marshes beckoning on the far side. The short walk down the river from the Mill Dam to the famous Bridge had a country air, and the dark Old Manse, where Ezra Ripley hatched out his hell-fire sermons, looked witch-haunted, even at high noon.

The best thing about Concord village, in Henry's estimation, was its smallness. A few minutes' jog trot in any direction brought him to fields, pastures, wood lots, swamps, and the unpeopled wildness in which the boy felt most at home. He yearned for wilder places than Concord offered.

Tameness to him meant dullness. He envied those first dwellers in this rich region of great lush meadows of never-mown grass when the whole country was their larder, supplying shad and shellfish and countless wild fowl. The air above them was thick with passenger pigeons at times.

They had called the stream Musketaquid, the Grass-ground River. Henry was pleased by the differences in the rivers so near his door—the Sudbury, idling from the south, broadened out into a grassy lake, with the Fair Haven heights looking down upon it; the Assabet, on the other hand, was a livelier stream, with clearer water; the Concord, formed by the union of the Sudbury and Assabet, offered a meditative course which it was one of the boy's ambitions to explore with his brother.

Glaciers had dumped hills here and there and Henry climbed them for views of the age-old Appalachian chain's first mountain—Wachusett, with Monadnock farther on. And as a final blessing, the native climate offered him more change, more exciting extremes, than a lifetime could appreciate. In summer, a tropic heat turned him into a fish in the Assabet's hemlock-shaded waters. In winter, he tasted the Arctic and became a bird on skates. Spring was teasing but enchanting; and autumn brought fruition of nut and harvest, with such fervent color as to transform his spirits into music.

Late in his life, Henry wrote in his Journal, "I have never got over my surprise that I should have been born into the most estimable place in all the world, and in the very nick of time, too." But even at fifteen, he had the ability to realize his good fortune. He had only to step outdoors to find the sort of country with which his nature could feel in complete harmony. His sense of identity with it was strong in him. It was as if he had a compact with nature, the only marriage bond he was to experience.

No wonder that he had a sense of independence. He felt that the boundless universe was his for the taking, and, instinctively, he was determined to spend his days in that enterprise. His vigorous, obstinate will, which his fellows often considered an infliction on them, was forming below the daily round of duties. This self-assurance was mainly his secret, but shown in jests, good-humored as yet, even practical jokes at his sisters' expense. It was not for eight years, when he was twenty-three, that he recorded his vow of integrity in words. He asked as pointed and fundamental a question as has been put to individuals: "If I am not I, who will be?" Who indeed? Gropingly, but steadily, he began to live a daily life that amounted to the only possible answer: *no one.*

David Henry Thoreau, as he was then called, was well on the way to being a person.

New Year's Day of 1833 brought in a spell of weather that reminded Cynthia Thoreau of the Cold Friday of her childhood, when water froze a few feet from the fire, and the family sat huddled in blankets, close to the hearth, all night long.

Henry loved weather, all weather, and listened to his neighbors' complaints of its deficiencies without sympathy. It was always too cold, too hot, too wet, too dry, or, if otherwise acceptable, too much the same to please the shop-keepers—who never got out in it—or the farmers—whose crops it always seemed to be damaging. Henry had learned the knack of being critical from his mother, and added to this the masculine talent, logic. He soon saw that the person whom the weather disappointed was really disappointing himself, or at least letting himself be disappointed. He could no more change it (thank Heaven) than he could change the calendar.

Henry's clear-sightedness did not make him popular, but, without planning to, he was acquiring the ability to see facts undistorted by prejudice, which was to make him unique and remembered. Years were to intervene before he could write down his views, years of mute suffering and hardship created by his sincerity. Yet the start was being made in the art of being oneself. Despite aunts, preachers, schoolmasters, and the hourly efforts of nearly everybody else to make him like others, he persisted in being Henry Thoreau, come what might.

Now that Helen and John were schoolteachers, in Taunton, Henry's chore was to get the family's day going by himself—chiefly by getting the fires started. A few live coals could be found in the raked-over ashes of the night before. Lifting a coal with tongs, he kindled a candlewick, which in turn kindled the shavings and small sticks already prepared. This small fire melted the ice in the kettle, and he carried the water, when hot enough, outdoors to thaw the wooden pump.

Henry liked to imagine himself an Indian, and in these early-morning encounters with the stern climate, he wondered how the Indians had ever managed to survive long spells of below-zero cold. His redskin counterpart had no ax, no saw, no stove, and the thinnest of shelters against the savage northeasters that could add ten inches of snow to the drifts from previous storms. Since the Indian kept no hens, he enjoyed no featherbed, no thick fluffy quilt such as Henry slept under in un-sachemlike comfort.

By the time that the boy had the pump working, the kitchen fire had begun to warm the room—and himself. He pumped water to fill the kettles on the pothooks over the flames. When the family came shivering downstairs, Henry savored the reward of his small sacrifice in their satisfaction. He was Yankee enough to wish to earn what he hoped to enjoy. Also, he liked working with his hands. Berries tasted better if he had picked them. The pencil he had helped make wrote more expressively than if bought. Long before his neighbor, Ralph Waldo Emerson, had delivered his lecture *"Compensation"* at the Lyceum, Henry had reached Mr. Emerson's conclusion by himself: *There is a price for everything.* And he knew you had to pay it.

True, the price tag was often concealed in daily life, but payment was exacted, either in advance—as when he had to labor with the fire before enjoying the heat—or basked later in the family's appreciation of his effort. Give-and-take formed an equation which you had better discover beforehand.

When Henry had gradually become aware of these underlying equations he kept running into instances of them everywhere. He understood the Reverend Ezra Ripley's sermons now. They were continually pointing out the rewards and punishments of conduct. "The wages of sin is death," seemed to be Dr. Ripley's favorite. Henry's mind was forever straying to life and its wages. At a cornhusking, you were after the corn, not the husks.

Presently the boy's silent acceptance of this compensation rule began to affect his daily thoughts and doings. He liked things easy, so he tried to keep them simple. Most people liked things easy, too, and complained because they were not. Yet they made life difficult for themselves by doing a lot of unnecessary things. Even the birds knew better! They built sound, useful nests and wasted no time on decorating them. His Concord neighbors worried themselves thin over decorating their houses. Henry looked with amusement at the absurd curlicues the architects glued onto porches. Suppose a catbird adorned itself with scarlet tanager feathers. How many birds would that fool? To be simple was to be sensible, in Henry's opinion. His mother called false fashion "putting on airs"—a good name for it, since it could be seen through like air, and its effect lasted little longer than the last breeze.

Henry remembered the day his own sister Sophia had apologized to a friend whom she had brought to see the arrowheads in his room, saying, "You must know, Amy, that my brother regards the dust on the furniture like the bloom on fruit: not to be wiped off on any account."

Girls' laughter didn't faze Henry. He was used to it. In his home, the teasing was affectionate. His family loved him and he loved them, and their differences mattered no more deeply than the wind ripples on the river mattered to its depths. On the Saturday night of that cold week, his satisfaction with the Thoreau home life led him to say, "Winter was made for families."

They were gathered close to the hearth, his father, mother, Sophia, and his father's sister Louisa, who was spending the winter with the Thoreaus. They missed Helen and John, at Taunton. The Saturday routine was accomplished, the house was clean, the bread and beans had been baked for dinner on Sunday—the day of no work.

On coming downstairs, Henry had found that his cat Min had lain on the bread dough, set out to raise, during the night, and caused it to raise all around her. "Scat!" he advised with a tickle of laughter. "I won't tell on you." It pleased him to be in league with his favorite animal. His only complaint of Min was that she disliked boating. Dogs would accommodate themselves to any vehicle that moved, but not cats. To be housed in a boat limited their independence. He could understand that and did not press voyages on Min.

One fruit of a family gathering was the solution of problems, or at least the discussion of them. Henry was halfway to sixteen, this January of 1833, and was beginning to enjoy argument for its own sake almost as much as did Cynthia of the tireless tongue. But he missed John, who usually backed him up. His father was too wise to breast the flood of women-talk. So Henry had to stand like a post in a stream, meeting the current, contradicting, and endeavoring to impose his budding masculine convictions on his opponents. It was perilous fun, especially when Aunt Maria joined the circle, for they all swooped on him like hen hawks.

Henry did not recognize the dangers of this wordy

warfare. It was gradually making him overly contentious and aggressive, and even somewhat contemptuous of others' views. At school, his habit of criticism was ill-taken. During recess, he did not play tag or blindman's buff or join in the ball game. Instead, he would sit on the schoolyard fence and fling caustic observations at his schoolmates' antics.

If a boy paid any attention to these unasked comments, he was soon laughing—or sore. For Henry's points were sharp and the reverse of what was considered common sense. He praised being alone, which everyone knew was boring. Or he said he liked to make a person angry because that way you got to know him as he was. Henry insisted that walking was better than riding, since you had a chance to see the country around you. He advocated abolishing carriages, so that people could see where they were going. These advices were so much a part of the growing, active-minded boy that he could not keep them to himself.

At school, his most irritating counsel concerned the Lyceum. When Henry was twelve, back in 1829, all Concordians interested in intelligent discussion met in the vestry of the Parish Church to hear Edward Emerson address a new society. Nine years earlier, a roving lecturer, who wanted to share his views, had spoken in the Brick Schoolhouse on the Square. His aim was to encourage like-minded people to meet at intervals for mutual enlightenment. This man, Josiah Holbrook, called such a meeting a Lyceum. Children of twelve were allowed to join the local Lyceum, and Henry promptly did just that. All the Thoreaus participated in the discussions and continued them in front of the home hearth. But when Henry urged his schoolmates to do the

33

same, they jeered at him. They preferred skating parties, taffy-pulls, and dances, to hearing more lectures from the elderly. They got enough of those at home.

Henry enjoyed dancing. Like his Uncle Charles, he was not averse to showing off his abilities, and fancy dancing was one of them. When Helen was at home to play the piano, Henry liked tootling his flute. Most unnatural of all, from his schoolmates' point of view, this Thoreau oddity actually *enjoyed* reading Greek and Latin and even French!

Henry brushed his critics aside. His tastes were an expression of his very being, and his satisfactions were solid and impervious to jeers. He knew he was no sissy. He could outwalk any boy his size, and outswim him, too. Also he could skate faster and farther, so what matter if he did look as funny as they said? He was a fair shot, a successful fisherman, and could handle a boat or canoe in a squall. He could ride a horse any distance, and drive a team. Once he was allowed to drive the six oxen that plowed out Main Street after a blizzard. He knew nature far better than Phineas Allen, the Preceptor, and could read the skies as accurately as George Minott, George Melvin, John Goodwin, or his own father.

Nor did he boast of his capabilities, although people called it boasting when he mentioned any one of them. Now that he was headed toward Harvard, he had additional reasons for sharpening his wits on the whetstone of the classics. Why was it that he enjoyed them so? He did not know precisely, but this he was sure of: he intended to pursue his personal joys. The sum of these was his happiness. Didn't the Declaration of Independence state that life, liberty, and the pursuit of happiness were the three good things? He felt so *alive* when he rejoiced, that to be joyous, in a sensible way, must be living aright. This he was determined to do, even if his advisers lined up in rows and made him run the gauntlet, as the Indians forced their captives to do. It was as fair a way to earn one's independence as any he could imagine.

Henry's birthday, July 12, fell on Friday, that year of 1833, and he had cause to remember it for years, because at 2 P.M., his father called to him that Marco Polo had escaped.

Henry had named their restive pig after the famed explorer because no enclosure suited him. Once before, he had escaped and proved such skill at dodging, charging, and other modes of eluding his pursuers, that Henry said, "Such pork ought to be called venison." On that first occasion he had had John to help him catch the beast.

Already, on that natal morning when he had become sixteen, Henry had performed several services for his family and he fervently desired to have the afternoon to himself. He planned to empty his boat of last night's downpour and explore the flooded river. A series of thunderstorms had lifted the usually placid stream out of its banks. Such a flood might not come again for years, and he was eager to mark its height on certain trees. Also, the sweep of the waters bore useful booty. It was nature's house cleaning, he had remarked, but Sophia had retorted, "A fine house cleaning that leaves everything twice as muddy as before!"

It was doubly necessary to have his afternoon to himself,

since the evening was to be wasted by going to a party. His sisters and the Hoar girls had planned to celebrate his birthday and his coming departure for Harvard with one of these gatherings which were marked by noise and social emptiness. Last spring, he had attended a similar goose-calling, as he termed it, because Sophia wished him to escort her and bring her home.

On the walk back, his sister had asked him how he had enjoyed it. "How desperate must one be before submitting a whole evening to such entertainment!" he had exclaimed. "The first girl I danced with was as jumpy and loquacious as a chickadee. She had been accustomed to the lively society of watering places and could get no refreshment from such a dry fellow as I. The next one was said to be pretty-looking, but I rarely look people in their faces, as you know and often blame me for, and I had no way of confirming the rumor. The third believed I could be won by compliments, but there was such a clacking that I could see only the motion of her lips and so missed hearing what a fine fellow I am. The fourth was as empty of thought as a cider pitcher in January, and I derive small pleasure from talking with a young girl half an hour simply because she has regular features."

"Oh, Henry!" Sophia burst into giggles. "You're just putting this on! I looked at you often and you were flushed with pleasure."

"That was the climate of those rooms. Nay, I always come to the same conclusion—the society of girls is the most unprofitable I ever tried. They are so light and flighty that you can never be sure whether they are really there or not."

"Haven't you ever found *any* girl you liked, Henry?"

"Why, yes. Last week I spent some hours with Miss Emerson. . . ."

"But, *Henry!* She's old enough to be your grandmother!"

"Nevertheless, she was perseveringly interested in wishing to know what I thought."

"So that's it!" Sophia exclaimed as they turned in at their gate. "We must hang on your words to seem attractive."

Henry did not contradict her, and Sophia stopped at the door. "Just you wait. One of these days you'll fall in love, and *then* we'll hear a different tune from you. But thanks for taking me. And tomorrow you can ask me whether I had a good time."

With that poke, Sophia vanished upstairs, and Henry felt the rebuke. He *was* self-centered, full of himself. His joys and plans and irritations occupied his thoughts. He must be badly to blame if it disturbed Sophia so. Yet was he not being honestly himself? Did they want him dishonest? Must he put on a false face, like the Halloween simpletons, to please them? He had determined to be Henry Thoreau with all his mind and body, and he wasn't going to be diverted from his course by some wisp of a girl. He would be lightweight indeed if a passing opinion could shift him about.

And now the dratted pig was forcing him to postpone his most cherished desire until it was caught and penned, and John, although home for the summer vacation, had gone to Lincoln on an errand!

Henry found his father inspecting Marco Polo's pen. "He's made a step of the trough and got out so," John senior said. "It must have been some time ago. Someday, Henry, I wish you'd make the pen deep enough to hold him."

"Only a well would do that," Henry said stiffly.

"I should not wish to keep him in a well."

Henry's quick ear caught the drollery of that objection and his mood softened somewhat. He must not take his unrest out on his good father. "Let's sell the pig, now, on the hoof, Father, as he runs, making a considerable reduction. Mr. Glenn was talking of buying a pig."

"I think we must make haste or else we'll lose him, Son."

Henry thrust the river out of his thought. Thanks to the rain, the shoat's tracks were easily followed. He weighed all of ninety pounds, and his hoofmarks led Henry along the edge of the garden, over the melons, through the beans and potatoes, and out under the gate, across the road, and along a ditch.

Henry jogged through the muck. The trail led steadily west. "A true American," Henry muttered. "I may catch up with him in Ohio!" The youth was getting back some of his accustomed wry humor, only to become irritated again: he had neglected to bring a rope to secure the swine when cornered.

The pig changed his mind about Ohio and swerved southward. The sultry air brought the sweat out on Henry, salting his eyes, tickling his back. He wished he could run clad only in a breechclout, like the Indians. But he knew that such common sense was beyond the conception of so-called civilization.

This reflection at civilization's expense put Henry in high spirits, and at the same time he spied Marco Polo, taking a mud bath in the street in front of Abby Palmer's. He ran faster.

"Shirttail's out, Henry," called Ray Chency, who was driving his team of oxen. "What you racing?"

Henry wasted no breath in replying. The pig had caught sight of his pursuer and bolted into Abby Palmer's front yard. Abby was digging in her garden, but on seeing the tusker heading for her, screamed and darted toward the house. Henry shut the gate behind him. The pig, now as alarmed as Abby, raced down the sloping lawn and crashed through the white paling fence, as if it were no obstacle whatever.

Henry heard Abby calling, "You'll pay for that, young man," but was too engaged to worry about costs. The pig had reached the street again, but was confused, turned in its tracks, and slithered around Henry.

"Ugly thing to catch," commented a bystander.

"You've got a job on your hands," said another.

"Whose is it?" asked a third.

"Ours," gasped Henry, who was running short of wind. The pig saw a team approaching and bolted into the Yarnall yard. Two boys joined Henry in the chase. "I could go an' git my uncle's dog," one boy volunteered. "Lives over to Carlisle. Won't take two hours. Three men can't catch a shoat in the open."

"He'll be in Boston in two hours," Henry flung back and trotted around the house, through the cow yard, and into a field of tall wet grass. He had a crowd of youthful helpers now. Henry's lungs were weary, though not his mind. He had to sympathize with the pig's urge to be free, and admitted that Marco Polo was no more obstinate than himself.

"I cannot but respect his tactics," Henry thought. "He will be he, and I will be I. He is not unreasonable because he thwarts me, but only the more reasonable. He has an oaken will. He stands upon his idea."

Having got back some wind and ease of mind, Henry neared a crowd in front of Colt's carriage shop. "He's in there," someone shouted. Henry and some boys hastened inside. Here he was able to borrow a rope. The livery space was crowded with carriages. The pig was resting his belly on the floor in the farthest corner and, according to Henry, thinking unutterable thoughts.

The chase recommenced within narrower limits. Knock, crack, bang, the pig went against wheels and shafts. He was all ear and eye. He stuck for a moment between the wide spokes of a cart wheel. Henry swooped and wound the rope rapidly around a hind leg. The pig squealed shrilly, but his appeal fell on hardened hearts. Henry and the boys dragged him out of the shop and the *driving* began.

It was all but hopeless. "Roll an egg as well," Henry said. Unnoticed, a black cloud had boiled up and now deluged the town with rain. The chief result was a little mud washed off pig and catcher. But now John reached them, with a wheelbarrow.

This was one enemy too much. By this time, Marco Polo was drained of energy. His captors wound the rope about him, lifted him upon the barrow, roped him on, and with three boys trudging along to make sure of no further accident, they got him home and into the pen.

Henry was wet through, caked with wheel grease, mud-stained, and tired to the bone. But he said he felt like Ulysses returning successfully from Troy. He felt so elated that even the ordeal of his birthday party ceased to damp his feelings. Before he went to clean up, he paid the indomitable pig no mean tribute. He said to John, "They ought to have him on our flag as symbol of the unconquerable will to freedom."

John burst into laughter at the idea of a pig adorning the Stars and Stripes and said, "I'll write to President Jackson tomorrow, conveying your recommendation, Henry. I don't doubt that he has chased enough pigs in his youth to sympathize with the idea."

It was the last of August, and on the morrow Henry was boarding the stagecoach for Cambridge, to enter the freshman class at Harvard University. He was homesick already. His head and heart were engaged in a taut tug of war. His intelligence pointed out clearly that he must further his education; his feelings attached him to the woods and waters of his Concord. Nothing he had heard of university life prepossessed him in its favor. Yet, like catching the pig, it had to be done. *Then* he could come back to Concord, a free man. It seemed silly to have to go through slavery to reach freedom; but there was no help for it, and Mr. Emerson had got him a scholarship.

On this still afternoon he was making the rounds of his favorite haunts, saying a farewell-without-words. He had saved Fair Haven Hill to the last. Already he had sat an hour watching the grand view toward the northwest and had made a heartfelt rhyme about Wachusett:

Wachusett, who like me
Standest alone without society—

When he had let that view sink in, he climbed higher and occupied his favorite lookout from Fair Haven Cliff. Below him, the river widened into a bay and the wild miles along the Sudbury stream were safe from the molestation of progress.

He sat there until the sunset faded, until the stars stood around dimly, in their everlasting safety. Thank Heaven, no misadventure could ever come to them.

THREE

College Boy

THE stage left Concord Square at 8 A.M. and took much of the day to cover the twenty miles to Cambridge, counting stops. Through the slow morning Henry's thoughts clung to his interrupted life: no cow to drive to pasture, no pig to feed—and pursue—no garden to hoe, nor berries to pick, nor fish to catch and bring home to his mother, no Minott to visit, nor Melvin to encounter in the woods, and worst of all, no brother John to laugh with and turn to for understanding and companionship. Henry felt an exile, and sympathized with the beaten Napoleon fastened up on that island. No wonder he had died twelve years ago. Henry remembered Dr. Ripley preaching on the pride of worldly might—for three hours.

During the afternoon, however, Henry's thoughts roved ahead. He knew himself well, and "know Myself" was what his Greek hero, Socrates, advised. He could endure. He had watched his father live from one disappointment to another without breaking. He, Henry Thoreau, had stood by his deepest convictions so far and would continue to be himself, whatever happened.

The jolts began when the freshman found that he must

43

room with two other students in Hollis. Good-by, privacy! He ate with five others at a commons table—and such food as he would have preferred to carry out to the pig. Mother Cynthia's meals had spoiled him for these second-rate messes. And the talk of these gentlemen! It was less decorous than the stable boys' ribaldry at the Concord livery. The interest of some of his classmates seemed less concerned with the curriculum than with games, cockfights, fancy women, and drink! Or so the lonely self-engrossed youth appraised them out of his inexperience.

A noisy few expected him to laugh at their practical jokes, go to the play, and dress in style. But he had only one suit. Its homespun coat of green had an orchard look, and when he attended chapel, he found himself surrounded by young gentlemen attired in black. They stared at him. He had broken their first rule—he had made a spectacle of himself.

They were also vastly amused by his nose. "You should have been a bald eagle," his brother John had once complained. "You've got the beak already." Henry could take jokes from John, who would have plunged through fire for him. But he read disdain in the glances of these well-groomed university grandees, most of whom could stare down at him. Henry stood five-feet-six and his chin did recede. His other features, however, fitted his nature. His deep-set, blue-gray eyes were piercing in their gaze, and it was his custom to avoid fixing them on people. His forehead was high, his hair brown, and, thanks to a vigorous life outdoors, his spare frame was sinewy and strong. Cynthia had tried to put some fat on him, but he walked it off. His arms were as strong as a stevedore's and his legs tireless.

44

Since Henry was so resistant to fashion, and since his habitual reserve made new attachments difficult to come by, he retreated into himself. Even if he had had money to spend, his shyness and his already settled sense of values would have kept him from frivolities and dissipation. His morals built a wall around him, nor did he try to find friends among the other poor and studious and sober boys in his class. His inexperience at mixing with others unfortunately hindered his making the acquaintance of some undergraduates whom he would have enjoyed.

Richard Henry Dana, who was soon to write *Two Years Before the Mast,* was one of these. James Russell Lowell might have become his friend; and Theodore Parker, with whom Henry was to share German lore later, would have befriended him. He did walk home, after six weeks of homesickness, with Stearns Wheeler, also of Concord. During this prolonged jaunt, which Henry had to finish in his stocking feet, he got his complaints about life at Harvard off his chest, and so his family did not have to bear the full brunt of his inflamed feelings.

Henry's eyes lighted when he was aroused, and they shone as he told the home circle about his discoveries in the Harvard Library, where he had forgotten his social solitude by hobnobbing with the great minds of all time. Henry rather unfairly complained that his schooling under Phineas Allen at the Concord Academy had "fitted or rather made him unfit" for college, for he was already so adept at Greek and Latin that he could read those ancients as his father read the newspaper. He used their yardstick of culture to sound his own depths and help remove the shallows of his thinking.

The priceless years from 1833 to 1837 added new dimensions to his village-born life.

This debt to the Harvard Library was to end only with his life, since he borrowed from its shelves for the rest of his years. He could have made a gainful use of his instructors, also, had he taken a wider view of individuality. But his loyalty to his own rigid limits was well-nigh deathless. Opposition merely made him the more obstinate. He *enjoyed* being his knotty self. It gave him pleasure to stand up against convention. Henry drew his own brand of joy from combating the established mode and the shocks that his paradoxes administered.

When his already famous English teacher, Professor Edward Tyrrell Channing, set the topic "Barbarism and Civilization," Henry seized this opportunity to be direly himself and showed why civilization should be abolished:

"The civilized man is a slave of Matter. Art paves the earth, lest he soil the soles of his feet; it builds walls, that he may not see the Heavens; year in, year out, the sun rises in vain for him; the rain falls and the wind blows, but they do not reach him. From his wig-wam of brick and mortar he praises his Maker for the genial warmth of a sun he never saw, of the fruitfulness of an earth he disdains to tread upon. . . . Our Indian is more of a man than the inhabitant of a city. He lives as a man, he thinks as a man, he dies as a man." The civilized man, Henry stated, "may spend days in the study of a single species of *animalculae,* invisible to the naked eye, and thus become the founder of a new branch of science—without having advanced the great objects for which life was given at all. The naturalist, the chemist, the mechanist, is no more a man for all his learning. Life is still as short as ever, death as inevitable, and the heavens as far off."

Henry felt good the night he rounded off that death knell to civilization, regardless of what the impressive Professor Channing would mark with his red pencil. He felt good because he was uttering his "I" with force and integrity. He was taking his first public steps, however unsteady they seem now, on that path of rugged individualism which was to lead him to this country's Hall of Fame a century and a quarter later.

He paid the usual price. The baffled Channing would not mark his pupil highly because Henry refused to swallow his rules of contemporary culture. Channing proposed that Henry should discipline himself to think out an idea until it assumed a logical form and was expressed precisely. Henry's mind worked poet-fashion. It was intuitive, operating by insights. The reasoning might come later, but he felt a power of recognition without recourse to inference. Throughout his life, Henry Thoreau's desire was to be "thought into." That was why the stillness of solitude was necessary for him. He must have time to lay his mind open to the sudden idea that might alight upon it, as a bird alights on a bough.

His long delvings in the Harvard Library had shown him that much work had to be done on a subject before it invited inspiration, just as a field must be plowed and let stand under the heavens before it is sown. At Cambridge, he missed the long solitary walks that abetted reflection. The notes dictated to him by his professors seemed secondhand in comparison with the jottings outdoors, where the professor was nature and life itself spoke daily from the rostrum of homely deeds and conflicts.

Pretty soon Henry was ignoring the student life about him. He did not know that he was being observed by a fellow classmate, John Weiss, who was to describe Henry in detail thirty years later. He mentions Thoreau's "tranquil indifference to college honors," and says, "He passed for nothing, it is suspected, with most of us; for he was cold and unimpressible. . . . He did not care for people; his classmates seemed very remote. This reverie hung about him, and not so loosely as the odd garments which the pious household care furnished. Thought had not yet awakened his countenance; it was serene, but rather dull, rather plodding. The lips were not yet firm; there was almost a look of smug satisfaction lurking around their corners. It is plain now that he was preparing to hold his future views with great setness, and personal appreciation of their importance."

There is Henry Thoreau, in chrysalis—the village boy in a town environment, different, rather uncouth and ungainly and open to ridicule, taking no pains to be popular. He willingly paid the price of neglect for the joy of being let alone. Inwardly, he began to be kindled by the literary giants in the Library and presently by an electrifying stranger whose rebellious mind struck a note that made Henry tingle. The first rip appeared in the chrysalis.

This encounter came about because, in Henry's junior year, 1835, he needed money. Expenses beyond the family's ability to pay prodded the eighteen-year-old student. He could be severely practical in an emergency, and since Harvard allowed a needy student one leave of absence to teach school, he accepted a position at Canton, not far from Boston. This meant forsaking his refuge, the Library. Also it meant facing seventy pupils. But the country youth had courage, and in the Reverend Orestes A. Brownson, who had examined him for the post, he found an individual who opened a new chapter in his life.

Brownson was large of frame, young in spirit, earnest, forward-looking, and as critical of the world as his protégé. Also, he was bursting with revolutionary ideas of what to do about it. The two sat up till midnight, exchanging views. Henry was having his first direct contact with a freethinker who burned to change society. Brownson was similarly delighted to find a disciple.

Thus began a period of forced growth for the river-dreamer who faced his classes with confidence born of a new power. His Harvard classmates would have stared in amazement at their recluse, who walked with lowered eyes, suddenly afire with Brownson's rash and untried plans for waking up a sleeping world.

The clergyman probably never knew Henry's inmost motives, for the Concord nature lover had no militant desire to reform the world or any part of it. His central idea was the reverse of wholesale reform. He had watched the farmers and shopkeepers plod through the year like so many sleepwalkers, oblivious of the earth's glory all about them. He wanted them to share his delight in the earth, water, and sky. They were slaves of routine, and he saw that they had to win a certain amount of freedom before they could delight in the pleasures at their doors, as he did.

Cambridge life was little better. When Henry discovered

the shallowness (in the Thoreauvian sense) of his class-mates' lives and ambitions, he determined to avoid *that* fate. What Brownson did for Henry was to show him that this sort of person did exist. The boy who, at fifteen, had rebelled against imprisonment in a house through a sunny Sunday because of an antique custom, had found a fellow rebel on a higher plane. As he wrote the country minister later, those six winter weeks "were an era in my life—the morning of a new *Lebenstag*"—a new day of living.

Henry became so overenergized by his new birth into the world of luminous ideas that he fell sick and missed months of college. But home was his cure. From April until autumn of 1836, he could float on his loved river, grow strong on Cynthia's cooking, and relax in the affectionate warmth of family life. He and John built a boat to succeed the *Rover*, their old square-ended craft. They painted a red stripe around the hull and christened the new craft *Red Rover*.

John, back from his own teaching with a larger view of the world, was antidote to any ill. John, however, wanted something more—some girl to take boating. He wrote to a like-minded friend at Woburn, "There is nought here save a few antiquated spinsters, or December virgins, if you will, and well may I sing 'What's this dull town to me? No girls are here.'" John was maturing, too. If he showed this note of protest to Henry, no comment on it has been saved.

Henry was not entirely averse to feminine society, though aware that he lacked John's ability to flatter and flirt for the passing amusement of both parties. If he envied John's playfulness, he allowed none to guess it. He lived life in his preferred fashion, rarely swerving, and so became his ideal-

50

ized self, in desire, thought, and act, with such thoroughness that he seemed singular to his neighbors. He has stood out against time, ever since, never merging with the mass, as roundedly sincere as any character in history.

The family knew that Henry had attained full health after the joke he played on Sophia. She had asked her brother to escort her to an afternoon party. She was dressed up in hoops and crinoline, a sweet and starchy sight. The day was hot and Henry suggested a short cut across a recently mown field. He even offered to hold her parasol, which was so unusual a piece of gallantry on his part that Sophia should have suspected danger.

He took her arm with his free hand, and they strolled across the field, which was alive with grasshoppers. By the time they had reached the far side, Sophia's hoop skirt had collected scores of the lively insects.

"Now look what you've done!" she exclaimed crossly to her brother. "Help me pick them off, the horrid things!"

"Why, you've discovered a principle!" Henry explained as he helped disengage the creatures from her dress. "Would this not be an excellent way to assist the farmers? To send a bevy of fashionably dressed young ladies across the field and wait until they got home to clean their skirts. It would soon rid whole acres of the pest and supplant anything at the patent office—and the motive power is cheap!"

"Oh, you!" Sophia complained. "All you think of is principles."

"It is not a common failing," her brother said, concealing his mirth.

This time, Henry felt more reluctant to leave home for college than three years earlier, but for different reasons. Then he had been a callow dreamer, only dimly aware of the real Henry. Now, thanks to Brownson's rap on his mind and heart, he saw into his identity with growing clearness, and his last year at college loomed as an obstruction to further realizing himself. He could not know that a much more profound stimulus was awaiting him.

Passing by a shop window in Cambridge, Henry caught sight of a small book entitled *Nature.* The title arrested his nature-starved eye, and to think that its author was Ralph Waldo Emerson, who lived only ten minutes' walk from his home! Henry had often seen Emerson on the way to the post office and liked that scholar's face, a little smooth perhaps, but genial, and highbrowed, as befitting a scholar. It had not mattered then to the young man that the Emersons and Thoreaus lived on different levels of Concord society. But if he and Emerson had nature in common, that was more to the point than afternoon teas.

Henry, with no money in his pocket, stepped into the shop, asked if he could inspect the book, and read the first sentence: "To go into solitude, a man needs to retire as much from his chamber as from society."

"True!" Henry concurred, and read on. "The lover of nature is he whose inward and outward senses are still truly adjusted to each other; who has retained the spirit of infancy even into the era of manhood."

"How very true!" Henry was excited. Why, here, in this neighbor, was a brother, closer than John in a way, for John could not have uttered Henry's own thought so clearly. "The spirit of infancy!" How his Harvard classmates would haw-

haw at that! Call it childhood, then, the time of pure hearts and innocent intentions. "Of such is the Kingdom of Heaven," thought Henry, remembering Ezra Ripley's last sermon. Morning joy was strongest and best, and boyhood was life's morning. That he would cling to. And here, in Mr. Emerson, he had a neighbor speaking his own truth. "The currents of the Universal Being circulate through me; I am part or parcel of God." That was it; that was what he felt alone, listening at evenfall to the thrushes in Thrush Alley.

Henry hurried to his room, counted his change, had enough to go back and buy the book, and read it as he trudged the familiar street. "I am the lover of uncontained and immortal beauty. In the wilderness, I find something more dear and connate than in streets and villages."

There he was in print! Mr. Emerson might have written those words in blood drawn from his Thoreau veins. They were his thoughts, and expressed the emotions he had felt at exalted moments on Fair Haven Cliff, or floating down the Sudbury, or walking naked on the bottom of the clear-as-air stream of the Assabet on a sultry August day.

From that day of discovery on, Mr. Emerson's pages fortified Henry in himself—in a part of himself, at least. Only the smallest part, of course. What he must do now was to set the rest of him down, just as truthfully, in cannonball sentences that could pierce the ribs of unbelievers and occupy their hearts. On this day he had been indeed reborn. How could he mark this second birthday? By giving himself a new name that would forever remind him of this lifting up. Dr. Ripley had christened him David Henry Thoreau. Henceforth it should be Henry David Thoreau.

That evening Henry began copying down some of the

Emersonian truths: "The health of the eye seems to demand a horizon." A new idea. He paused to consider this view of a fact he had never looked at thoughtfully enough.

"We are never tired, so long as we can see far enough." He had felt that, without realizing it in so many words. He would climb Mount Washington again and test the idea.

"Beauty is the mark God sets upon virtue." Henry stopped to reflect on that. What was virtue, exactly?

He was too stimulated to linger over definitions and read on: "A man's power to connect his thought with its proper symbol and so to utter it depends on the simplicity of his character, that is, upon his love of truth and his desire to communicate it without loss."

Henry drew back instinctively from this flood of pronouncements. He felt like saying, "Go more slowly, my friend." He would have to weigh those statements in the light of the utterances by great men shed upon him in Harvard's library. But he was won by that word *simplicity*. It was the signboard on the road to happiness, as plain as the wooden hand on the Boston Post Road. He knew that. He had watched the grown men of Concord drudge away from dawn to dark, and after dark, to pile up the encumbrances that buried the simple life, until the very idea of freedom had been lost sight of. If Mr. Emerson wished to start with simplicity of character, he had company in Henry David Thoreau.

It was past midnight before Henry had finished penciling comments beside the paragraphs of *Nature*. He felt reinforced. He was surer than ever that he knew where he stood with himself and with the everyday world. Emerson had focused the light in him to a burning point. In that light he saw clearly what he wanted to live for: it was to *be*—to know that he was a *living* being. He admitted, drowsily now, that reducing multiple life to a simplicity would be as difficult as proving truth.

He woke next morning to more particular facts. Would he ever be able to exchange thoughts with Mr. Emerson, who did seem rather withdrawn, almost haughty in a gentle way? Dare he tell the older man that he approved of his writings and wished to discuss them? Even if refused that intimacy, it would be a continuing joy to know that he had an unseen friend there on Lexington Road who would approve of his reinforced vow: to be—to be himself—to be as much himself as he could give life to—above all, to be simple, to keep coming back to simplicity. That was it.

Henry's revolutionary ardor showed itself to the astonished audience that gathered to hear the Commencement speeches on August 13, 1837. When the new Henry David Thoreau mounted the platform, his distinguished hearers saw a rather short but not stumpish youth of twenty, with Caesar's nose and the American eagle's intense eyes, clad in somewhat rustic garments, with plenty of brown hair brushed aside from a scholar's brow. They heard a voice, strong in its self-confidence, and suddenly they sat up tensely while the voice uttered these preposterous sentences as if they were the kernel of truth:

"This curious world which we inhabit is more wonderful than it is convenient; more beautiful than it is useful; it is to be more admired and enjoyed than used. The order of things should be somewhat reversed; the seventh should be man's day of toil, wherein to earn his living by the sweat of his brow; and the other six his Sabbath of the affections and the soul—in which to range this widespread garden, and drink in the soft influences and sublime revelations of nature."

There, he thought, *I have said it.* As he walked to his seat, the applause was scant. Clearly the young man was unbalanced, if not sacrilegious, turning God's arrangements upside down, advocating work on the Lord's day and loafing for the rest of the week. Why let such a confused student speak, much less graduate? Did Harvard University confer a degree for such nonsense as that?

Emerson, who was lecturing at Harvard that year, was undoubtedly in the audience, and recognized a disciple. He consulted the program: Henry David Thoreau. Yes, of course, the Concord boy he had got the scholarship for. He had made worthy use of it. He must keep an eye on the young man. Certainly he had a forthright style, as well as fresh thought. The country could do with more such graduates.

Henry, peculiar as ever, refused to get drunk with his class, and skipped, rather discourteously, President Josiah Quincy's reception. He couldn't get back to Concord fast enough. Thanks to the Library, Brownson, and *Nature,* he had grown a good four years' worth during his difficult stay at the University. And now he was free, *free.*

FOUR

A New Thing in Schools

THE day after Henry's return from Cambridge he felt light and released and enjoyed a reunion with his rivers and woods. "My thoughts are my company," he told the busybodies who questioned his independence. His thoughts were indeed the individuals he could count on meeting the moment he was alone. They never failed him, as people so often did. Thought produced thought in a linked chain, and he was surprised by the newness of the thought at the end of a sequence. He made a habit of leaving old thoughts at home, when he went for a walk, so that fresh ideas could enter his mind freely. To be "inspired" was truly to be "breathed into."

Some of his inspirations were worth preserving, and Henry recalled a topic given him by Professor Channing for an essay: "Of Keeping a Private Journal, or Record of Our Thoughts, Feelings, Studies and Daily Experiences—containing abstracts of Books, and the Opinions we formed of them on first reading them."

By coincidence, in October, Emerson met Henry on the Mill Dam and asked whether he was keeping a journal. "I myself have kept one for years," the older man said, "and find it invaluable. Anyone aspiring to a literary career, or even to a private expression of what existence in this world means to him, can hardly get along without such a record of experience, inner or outer."

Henry thanked Mr. Emerson and at once bought a blank book in a red binding. That evening he began the gigantic labor which was to produce fourteen huge volumes, totaling six thousand pages, to become American literature's largest opus and perhaps its greatest.

Henry's opening confidences were typically Thoreauvian: "To be alone I find it necessary to escape the present—I avoid myself. How could I be alone in the Roman Emperor's chamber of mirrors? I seek a garret. The spiders must not be disturbed, nor the floors swept, nor the lumber arranged."

His thirst for solitude, after the enforced mingling with the crowd at Cambridge, led him to copy down other poets' longings for the same sort of retirement.

Herbert advised:

> Salute thyself; see what thy soul doth wear
> By all means use sometime to be alone.

Burton was just as emphatic:

> Friends and companions, get you gone!
> 'Tis my desire to be alone;
> Ne'er well, but when my thoughts and I
> *Do domineer in privacy.*

And Marvell summed up this joy:

A NEW THING IN SCHOOLS

Two Paradises are in one
To live in Paradise alone.

Unfortunately, one had to live *on* something, even when alone, and that meant earning cold cash. So, even during his walks, Henry turned over in his mind the possibilities of lucrative employment which would least interfere with his resolve to be himself.

When he put the question to his mother, she said, "You can buckle on your knapsack and roam abroad to seek your fortune."

But this was intolerable! Hadn't he just got home? His sister Helen, seeing the distress in her brother's face, threw her arms about him and said, "No, Henry, you shall not go! You shall stay at home and live with us!"

Yes, but what on? His family had made sacrifices for four years to keep him at Harvard. Now he must at least earn his way. He was willing to use his hands, but not at a routine job like pencil making, which killed the poet in one. He could lay walls, repair doors, even clean out chimneys; the point was to have free time for scouring Concord for thoughts.

Cynthia loved her knotty son too warmly to press the point and Henry stayed home. He helped the family move into the Parkman House, which offered more space for boarders, whose money was welcome to manager Cynthia. A Mrs. Ward, the widow of a colonel in the Revolution, and her daughter were congenial guests.

Henry, however, felt submerged in women. What with the Wards and aunts and female cousins continually at the table, the feminine chatter got on his bachelor nerves. He had grown more assertive, thanks to Brownson's example and Emerson's precepts in *Nature*. Sometimes he stated these startling beliefs in a way that made kindly quiet Helen question her loving impulse to harbor Henry under the family roof.

" 'Man is a dwarf of himself,' " Henry quoted and looked around to see who dared differ. Aunt Louisa's eyebrows rose; she did not feel like a dwarf.

" 'Man is a god in ruins,' " Henry went on, echoing Emerson again, but out of context. Mr. Thoreau stared at his collegiate son, but was too gentle to express his doubts. Cynthia barely held her active tongue. Sophia laughed nervously at such nonsense, and hoped they had not made a mistake in sending their nice Henry to that horrid university. John grinned at the welcome commotion that Henry's newfound philosophizing was creating, and asked his family if they wanted Henry to come back from Harvard unchanged.

Helen was ever the most embarrassed when Henry "showed off," as she termed his intellectual antics, and apologized to the guests. This wrung an angry explanation from Henry, who wished his sister to understand that he was "revealing" and not "showing off." His hurt went deep and he wrote to a friend, complaining that gross injustice was being done to him by Helen's obtuseness.

Another mannerism of his had grown during the college years. When he was concentrating on the object of his thought, he did not let his eyes rove on the multiplicity of faces, signs, and ugly edifices about him. For some reason, it bothered the person he was talking to if he did not stare in

that person's face. Nor did he like being stared at and explained why: "It's said that a rogue doesn't look you in the
face, nor does an honest man look at you as if he had his reputation to establish. I've seen some who didn't know when
to turn aside their eyes in meeting yours. A truly confident
and magnanimous spirit is wiser than to contend for this
mastery in such encounters. Serpents alone conquer by the
steadiness of their gaze. My friend looks me in the face and
sees me, that is all." One infers that Henry preferred not to
be a serpent.

In Concord village and township, the new university graduate was offered a variety of employment. But Henry
shunned being housed in offices during daylight hours. He
made one effort to sell pencils, but he lacked the smiling approach to possible customers that salemen must cultivate. Integrity was one of his unwritten names that he would not
change. He had grown up without losing the truth of his
nature and proposed to remain unwaveringly himself. He
offered his services for sale, but never himself. The unsym-
pathetic observer might call him smug but not false. He was
determined not to make the kind of fool of himself that he
judged he saw around him—those who sold their present liberty for future happiness. His policy was to make sure of the
happiness.

Yet he was sensitive as well as honest, and so he was
hounded on his walks by the yap-yap of his conscience—he
must earn. His proposed week of Sabbaths with only one day
set aside for remunerative toil began to seem rather vaporish
and too far ahead of the times, after all. He recalled the one
activity by which he had earned money without smirching

his conscience: pedagogy. On the eve of the new year, 1838, he wrote to Orestes Brownson, saying that he wished to teach. He was explicit on one point: he was anxious to make education pleasant to teacher and scholar alike. He considered that the instructor should be a fellow student with his pupil, learning of him as well as teaching him.

This astounding idea must have made Brownson rub his eyes. In those days, the schoolmaster was autocrat and enforced discipline with a whip. Henry rebelled at the sight of a boy being birched because he could not spell. What stupidity on the master's part to suppose that fear was the right incitement to true learning!

With his usual humor, Henry wrote Brownson that "the cowhide is a nonconductor, unlike the electric wire," and unable to transmit a spark of truth to the slumbering intellect it would address.

Henry did not have to wait until Brownson hunted up an opening for him. Concord's elementary school for younger children needed a teacher, and Henry backed up his application with three high-quality letters of recommendation:

Harvard's President wrote that Mr. Thoreau's rank "was high as a scholar in all branches, and his morals and general conduct unexceptional and exemplary." He had forgotten or forgiven Henry's cutting his reception for the graduating class. "He is recommended as well qualified as an instructor for employment in any public or private school, or private family."

The Reverend Ezra Ripley, whose word was law in Concord, also recommended Henry, saying, "He is modest and mild in his disposition and government, but not wanting in energy of character and fidelity to the duties of his profession."

Ralph Waldo Emerson wrote of him, "An excellent scholar, a man of energy and kindness, and I shall esteem the town fortunate that secures his services."

The twenty-one-year-old youth felt so confident with such backers that he announced in advance that he would not flog but talk morals as a punishment instead. Henry's Journal is silent on what followed. Did the youngsters, when relieved of fear, take advantage of this soft duck, who chided but whipped no one, and cut up? Or did the pupils take home magnified stories of this innovation and scandalize their parents with its absurd lenience? Or was Henry's method of preaching punishment too inexplicable for the habit-ridden overseers to swallow?

Only a fortnight had passed before Henry was irritated by a visit. A thin-lipped deacon with a rocky chin strode into the classroom and accepted Henry's chair. The young instructor taught on, making the subject under discussion live because he put his heart into it. The deacon mistook the children's easy manner and impetuous interest for crass misbehavior. He was accustomed to pupils sitting like graven images, and believed, like Solomon before him, that a spared rod guaranteed a spoiled child. Presently he delivered an ultimatum, "Mr. Thoreau, this won't do. You must flog or the school will spoil."

Henry was quickly aroused by injustice, and obstinate when he considered himself in the right. If he yielded to the old fossil, who could not see that a happy child learned better than a sullen one, he would keep his job. He was enjoying it and it seemed to him the one way of earning without roweling his conscience. But Henry could no more soil himself by that sort of treachery than sell himself to shopkeeping. So he said to the committeeman, "How can raising a welt on a child's skin increase his desire to learn?"

"Order is essential for getting the lesson."

"There is order, there is attention, even enthusiasm, even joy. They are learning, not by rote but with eagerness."

"Mr. Thoreau, employ the ferule or resign."

Henry's temper was aroused. "Then keep the school yourselves, for I will not brook interference."

He dismissed the astonished scholars, and, to drive his point home, lined up six of them, one of the six being the maidservant at his home, and applied the ferule, with a sharp smack on the right hand of good or poor student alike.

The outraged youngsters were now as indignant as their master. They could not know that they were being sacrificed to a principle. On reaching home, Henry found that the maid had aroused the family.

Cynthia burst out with, "Jane has shown me her smarting hand and told a strange tale. Henry, can it be that you have punished her for no wrongdoing?"

"Yes, Henry, pray explain," Aunt Louisa interrupted. "I have just returned from the Mill Dam, where I heard much resentment."

Henry reported the deacon's intrusion and his dullness in confusing the pupils' rather noisy interest with disorder. "I could not revert to flogging, particularly after I had announced that I would not flog. So I had to withdraw—but not before I had given the school committee an object lesson."

"What lesson?"Aunt Louisa asked sharply. "I must be as dull as the deacon, since I cannot comprehend why you could whip a good girl like Jane, who thinks the world of her teacher. Poor dear, she is in tears, not from the hurt but for her fallen hero."

"I wished to show that physical punishment and scholarship have naught in common," Henry replied stubbornly.

"Then you fell into your own trap!" Cynthia exclaimed. "Your aim to convince the committee by rapping innocent knuckles lacks logic, Son. I much fear that this will not end quickly."

"I tell you it has ended, so far as I am concerned."

"After all this search for the suitable work?" Cynthia was distressed as well as angry.

"Perhaps a polite letter of apology . . ." began Aunt Louisa.

"Apologize for being right?" Henry asked cuttingly.

Brother John had kept quiet. He was too fond of Henry to upbraid him for this nonsense. But now he felt it necessary to come to Henry's assistance, so he said, "Can't you see, Mother, that Henry has sacrificed his safety for a principle? This is precisely what Concord has prided herself on doing since the Fight at the Bridge. And now Henry precipitates a similar revolution for justice' sake—and just as valuable a liberty, if you ask me. Concord's battle for principle begat the United States of America. Henry's battle for principle may help do away with the senseless flogging of backward children, who need patience and understanding instead. Let's have supper."

John Thoreau, Senior, ever closemouthed in that household of bristling opinions, now said, "I think John has the right of it on both counts. Henry could not keep his position against his conscience, and we'll all feel better after we've eaten." Then he looked at his younger son and added, "Tell Jane you were re-enacting Concord Bridge and that she now is history. It will salve her feelings."

The family were drawn together during the next few days, to form a shield against the village's sharp criticism of Henry. Concord was used to making allowance for its independent spirits, but Concord had already made up its mind that this Thoreau boy, who seemed to be a born idler, who preferred hobnobbing with vagrants like that One-eyed Goodwin, was destined to be a good-for-nothing, and soon turned its attention elsewhere.

This clash caused Henry to take a still narrower view of Concord society. He "signed off" the parish church, where Dr. Ripley had been preaching to him since childhood, because he objected to the tithes system and did not see eye to eye with certain of the Puritan beliefs. The minister was unaccustomed to having his hearers secede, and was affronted, as were Henry's aunts.

These misunderstandings irritated the ex-teacher to the point of considering leaving his beloved home again, in spite of an interesting new boarder at the Thoreaus' house—Mrs. Lucy Jackson Brown, who was no less than the sister of Emerson's wife Lidian. Her husband was away on business in Europe much of the time, and Lucy Brown enjoyed living only a few minutes' walk from her sister. She was fifteen years older than Henry, but listened with pleasure to his sharp comments on people and their peculiar customs, such as cooping themselves up in offices all their lives in order, sometime later, to live.

But even Lucy Brown could not take the sting out of the endless reproaches that Henry had to hear. With his sister Helen teaching music in Roxbury, and John managing a school in West Roxbury, Henry thought that he would find teaching elsewhere a good plan. Efforts were made by friends to obtain a position for Henry as far away as Louisville, Kentucky, and Bangor, Maine, where relatives of the Thoreaus lived, but these attempts were fruitless. Henry's resilient spirits soon came to his aid and he decided that, if John would return to Concord and help, they could start a private school right there in Concord and prove before everyone that his principle of persuasion was more effective than trying to thrash children along the road of learning.

John agreed gladly and Henry rounded up four boys from out of town to board at his home and be taught. The Parkman House was a spacious, white-painted frame dwelling, as dignified in appearance as Emerson's home. It was conveniently located at the junction of Main Street and Sudbury Road, where Concord's Library now stands.

Happiness is contagious, and boys will talk. So in a short while other children, girls as well as boys, persuaded their parents to let them attend the Thoreau school, where it was fun to study and no whip stood behind the door. Presently, the more intelligent families of Concord began to recognize the advantages in the new Thoreau method. They liked genial John. Soon the enrollment taxed the facilities of the Parkman House and the brothers leased the Academy nearby.

John Thoreau, now aged twenty-four, was business manager of their novel enterprise, and teacher of the sciences. Henry taught the classics and mathematics. Both brothers carried the friendliness of their home life into the schoolroom. They ruled by affection, tempered with a reasonable firmness, and they baited the curriculum with outdoor interests hitherto unheard of in schooling. John's gaiety and warmth of heart soon had the boys, in addition to the girls in love with him. He played marbles, showed them improved methods of top-spinning, handicapped himself at hopscotch by carrying the dictionary, and even prolonged recess to finish a game of blindman's buff. His example enabled them to see that all fun had to have a skeleton of discipline, and that punishment for misbehavior was just. He made it plain that he enjoyed the company of little boys but not *brats*.

Disobedience rarely reared its head because laughter was more fun. John and Henry were ready laughers, and Henry liked to poke fun at his charges. "Yesterday I saw one of those meddlesome dogs chasing some cows in the Hosmer pasture," he said one morning. "And I thought 'they are the dog state of those boys who pull down handbills in the streets. Those boys' next migration, perchance, will be into such dogs as those, an ignoble state.' Watch out!"

At another time, when Henry overheard a boy saying that he was going to catch a young owl and tame it, he quoted Blake's lines: "A Robin Redbreast in a cage/Puts all heaven in a rage." The boy, without further rebuke, gave up the project. He did not want all heaven in a rage at him.

Henry also had a novel way of curing the older boys from using the oaths they overheard in rough company and on the

68

street. The brothers prefaced each morning's work with a talk, and, one rainy morning, when Henry heard a fifteen-year-old redhead swearing like a sailor, he said, "Boys, if you want to talk business with a man, and he persists in thrusting words having no connection with the subject into all parts of every sentence—*bootjack*, for example—wouldn't you think he was taking a liberty with you and trifling with your time and wasting his own? For instance, if I say, 'the bootjack farmers in this bootjack place would be a bootjack sight better off if the bootjack climate wasn't so bootjack bootjack cold,' do you think that improves the meaning?"

The children laughed and agreed with Trainer Thoreau, as Henry was called. He knew that he was not popular, as John was, but so long as he was obeyed with alacrity and succeeded in transferring his knowledge to these pupils, he was happy.

The brothers' own experience at home had taught them that children appreciated being considered responsible. Accordingly, every pupil had some duty assigned to him or her, as on a sailing vessel. Eager pupils were especially desired, and the Thoreaus reduced the tuition for likely youngsters from homes where the parents had a hard time making ends meet. During the snowy months, when the mercury often stayed near zero, Cynthia took as many out-of-town boys to board as room allowed.

Later, one boy told Emerson's son, Edward, "Mrs. Thoreau's bread, brown and white, was the best I ever tasted. She had, beside, vegetables and fruit, pies and puddings; but I never saw meat there. At the home was nothing jarring.

Mrs. Thoreau was pleasant and talkative and her husband was kind. If I ever saw a gentleman at home, it was he."

The Thoreau food was good because the family raised much of it themselves. The home garden was Henry's responsibility. His specialty was melons; he cultivated sixty hills of them. He milked the cow, tended to the chickens, raised pigs as well as beans, the vegetable on which New England was founded.

Henry taught his classes in a large room on the second floor. One lowering day, the third of a tedious drizzle, a comparatively new boy, but the largest in the school, decided to get even for some rebuke that Trainer Thoreau had bestowed on him the day before, so he started to chew up a page of newspaper with spitballs in view.

Henry was explaining a geometry problem at the time. His rather triangular nose gave him a stiff expression. When immersed in his work, Henry could be as direct and uncompromising as any theorem that Euclid was determined to prove. His way of teaching differed from John's. While John managed to ease the tension caused by a reciter's fumblings and mistakes by some sympathetic remark, Henry kept his mental eye on the work before him, wasting no time or words. The pupil was forgotten in Henry's concentration on the lesson.

Upon the blackboard which Henry had constructed, he had drawn a large circle, round and perfect as the full moon. As he stepped back to regard it, a pulpy wad of spitball splashed against the blackboard at almost the exact center of the circle. The hit was so precise that the class sucked in its breath sharply, admiring the skill of the blow, and wondering how Trainer would punish the fresh boy, who stood three inches taller than Master Henry, and who would have been given a severe thrashing from any teacher they had known previously.

Henry faced about unhurriedly. His glance had taken on the blue light of cold steel. "A bull's-eye," he observed crisply. "Such marksmanship should not go unnoticed," nor was the double meaning of "unnoticed" lost on the tense pupils. Henry had marked the guilty party without difficulty and said, "Adam, the class will attend while you offer us an exhibition of your skill."

The class sat up more intently than ever, and a murmur of drawn breaths passed over the room, like a waft of air before a storm.

"Adam, make another spitball, if you please," Henry ordered.

The class was mystified. What *was* coming? Any other master would have been fiery mad, but Trainer's tightly pursed lips and fixed gaze expressed purpose rather than wrath. His short, erect figure actually appeared commanding, full of thrust, as he looked at the now embarrassed culprit. "If ready, rise."

Adam had found newspaper chewing suddenly distasteful, but he rose. "Now," Trainer said matter-of-factly, "I shall stand here as target. Fire your missile at my forehead. Plant it in the center as neatly as you did on my figure." Was that another pun, two or three of the brighter students wondered?

The class in general gasped, rigid now with expectancy. Adam towered, red of face, speechless. He had counted on Trainer's customary sarcasm to win the room's sympathy; now he was shaken by the absence of support. Henry's bearing, on the other hand, seemed molded by a self-respect as open and vigorous as manhood itself.

"Proceed," Henry commanded the paralyzed youth. "Aim well. I shall not flinch."

Crimson-faced Adam could not stir. "What detains you?" Henry demanded. "You won't do to my face what you did behind my back?"

A few half-suppressed titters showed that some had recognized Trainer's grim joke. "Fire away," he ordered.

"I can't."

"You mean I should move nearer?"

Adam swallowed and shook his head. "I can't, sir. I'm sorry, sir." Adam subsided into his seat.

"When a dog runs at you, whistle for him," Henry advised dryly. "Let us return to Euclid."

Such quixotic misunderstandings were rare, however, because the children responded to this novel school atmosphere of good will—and circuses. The brothers saw to it that much of their education went in by the side door. Henry's enthusiasm for Indian ways helped turn pedagogy into a pleasure. When humorous Oliver Wendell Holmes called Henry "half college graduate and half Algonquin," he was stretching the joke. But Henry had so keen a sympathetic knowledge of the wilds that he could think from the Indian point of view.

It was his skill at reasoning like a redskin that enabled him to locate camp sites of forgotten tribes and find the cooking utensils the squaws had used, old stone pestles in which maize was ground. He picked up so many arrowheads that he made a sort of half-Latin pun by calling the sands of these campsites *arrowheadiferous,* arrowhead-bearing. John reminded the youngsters that the inquisitive chickadees which flitted close to them when they ate lunch outdoors were descendants of chickadees that had poked their beaks into wigwams pitched on the same grounds by dusky squaws of a hundred years before.

This sort of teaching was new and looked forward to eagerly. "Love and they will learn" was the schoolmaster philosophy put into practice at the Thoreau school. The children did learn with astonishing thoroughness. The parents gladly paid the tuition for such success. It looked as if Henry had settled into his lifework at last.

FIVE

The River Trip with John

"DID you ever see a happier pair of brothers?" Cynthia Thoreau remarked to her husband.

Boarder Prudence Ward overheard and said, "Not since Cain and Abel—before the quarrel."

"They've had their differences but no quarrels," Cynthia put in.

Prudence's mother said, "How could two brothers be so different? John is uncomplicated, pleasant of nature, fond of everyone, especially the girls, and accepts affection from young and old without in the least being spoiled by it."

"Yes, that's John," his father concurred.

"But Henry!" Mrs. Ward made a gesture almost of despair. "So full of contradictions! He enjoys dancing, yet shuns society. He hasn't John's easy way with people, yet burrows into their minds, and is then at odds with what he finds there. He has outdistanced John in scholarship and the questioning of life. . . ."

"While withdrawing from it," Prudence declared. "He buries himself in a book on a winter night, as I do in bed, and pulls the covers over him."

"The book covers?" Cynthia laughed. "Why, you're as bad

74

at puns as Henry. But he withdraws from bores, Prudence. Only yesterday he told me that nothing was so tiresome as people lacking depth, who reported only what they heard from without, since they heard nothing within. He loves the other sort, the simple folk who are honest enough to think their own thoughts. They find Henry as sociable as John, though in a different way."

Prudence was not persuaded. "Since Henry began confiding in that Journal, we mere people hardly count. I suspect that talking to himself, with a pen, is the greatest satisfaction of his life."

Father John interrupted with, "Didn't you hear what Henry said this morning? That the question is not what you look at but what you *see*? Each of you sees a different Henry. Let the boy alone. I do not like these dissections of living individuals. Nobody is going to get to the bottom of Henry, or John either, over a teacup."

Thanks to Henry's success in teaching and his daily cooperation with John, he was experiencing a rare period of happiness. And soon he was to be happier. For in June of that year, 1839, a boy of eleven named Edmund Sewall came with his mother to visit the Wards and stayed at the Thoreaus' home. Henry had got acquainted with a wide range of boy character and was delighted by this amiable youth. Edmund had grown up by the sea and reveled in the woods and river in Henry's company. His appreciation of them won Trainer Thoreau.

By now, Henry's zest for analyzing people had developed into an exaggeration of approval, or disapproval, nurtured by his absorption of Emerson's *Nature*. Accordingly, he wrote down Edmund in his Journal as "a pure, uncompromising spirit, that is somewhere wandering in the atmosphere, but settles not positively anywhere," which is a rather overblown description of a certain sort of dreamy yet active boy. "Such it is impossible not to love; still is their loveliness, as it were, independent of them." Then comes the whole truth: "That virtue we appreciate is as much ours as another's. We see so much only as we possess."

There was artist Thoreau emerging—with a truth as old as poetry in his mouth. John could never have penned those observations. But Henry was not satisfied with putting his delight so briefly, and within two days had composed a long poem, a sensitive account of his feelings about Edmund. He lifted them above person into the philosophy slowly taking shape in his being.

He called his poem "Sympathy," and its spiritual beauty, so clearly set forth, must have encouraged the beginning poet, when he read it over, by its evidence of his ability to put his already subtle vision of the heart into verses justly. His own natural restraint stands behind the lines set down in the seclusion of his garret workshop:

> Lately, alas, I knew a gentle boy,
> Whose features all were cast in Virtue's mould,
> As one she had designed for Beauty's toy,
> But after manned him for her own stronghold.
> On every side he open was as day,
> That you might see no lack of strength within. . . .

The poem climbs above everyday considerations in the fashion of Concord's high thinkers of that time. Emerson's

prose had won Henry over to this idealistic mode of considering fact. In "Sympathy" he expresses contradictions which
tend toward paradox, that is Truth's stronghold, as in these
lines:

> So was I taken unaware by this,
> I quite forgot my homage to confess;
> Yet now am forced to know, though hard it is,
> I might have loved him, had I loved him less.
>
> Each moment, as we nearer drew to each,
> A stern respect withheld us farther yet,
> So that we seemed beyond each other's reach,
> And less acquainted than when first we met.

Had John been asked to comment on Edmund Sewall, he
might have said, "Ed's a good kid, nice to have around." But
Henry, with a poet's privilege, not only enjoyed Edmund's
company but set about measuring him by the yardstick of his
own perceptions and self-respect, thereby lifting both of them
above everyday concerns into the lasting reality of art. The
child was a springboard for Henry's idealizaion of pure love.

Henry, now twenty-two, had not yet been played upon by
beauty in the shape of a young girl. He would have been the
last to foresee what was about to happen when Edmund's
sister, Ellen Sewall, came with her mother from the seaside
town of Scituate, Massachusetts, to visit the Wards and
Cynthia Thoreau.

At seventeen, Ellen's beauty, reinforced by a charming nature, was enlivened by her delight in its effect on young men.
She captivated them as fast as they appeared. And if a boy

77

of eleven could elicit a poem from Henry, it was natural that Ellen should call forth two poems. John's competition for Ellen's attention woke the dormant sense of romance in Henry. The brothers took turns showing this appreciative damsel the sights of their leafy inland village.

John, with Prudence Ward as chaperone, walked Ellen to the famous North Bridge. Henry, without a chaperone, took her boating. He got ahead of John by escorting her to see a traveling show with its elephants and exotic giraffe, and doubled her up with his jokes. He and Ellen talked Dickens, who lay beyond John's scope, and Henry was happy to find that this lovely girl had a receptive mind. He was on the crest of a new joy, with a wider view of earth and heaven than Fair Haven Hill had ever given him, and wrote in his Journal, "Nature doth have her dawn each day," but his own dawns were brighter.

This charmer from afar had indeed ushered in a new day for bachelor Henry. He was in love. But so was John, who was physically more prepossessing, and who had had more practice in the art. Also, John was twenty-five and his attentions flattered the young girl, who could not help but exercise her charm on all comers. In a matter of days, despite boating and giraffe, John had taken a long lead. Henry, the slighted, had to fall back on his Journal for company. It was then, in the depths of heartache and envy, that he penned this admonition to all unsuccessful lovers: "There is no remedy for love but to love more."

Youth's torment had elicited from him one of the truest and most beautiful outcries uttered by a brave spirit in love against odds. If Willliam Shakespeare, at twenty-two, had

78

begun, or ended, a poem with that line, it would be quoted by all civilized people. Emerson was writing another version of its truth in another house down the road: "Love and you will be loved"—not by the loved person, perhaps, but by another yet unmet and worthier of one's love.

Henry's immediate fate was to watch John monopolize the enchanting girl until he had no heart left for Journal confidences. For five weeks no word was penned. Then the Sewalls left Concord. Almost at once, on August 31, 1839, the two brothers embarked on a trip down the Concord River and up the Merrimack, an excursion long planned.

A few weeks earlier, Henry had been counting on a fortnight alone with John in the craft they had labored hard to make riverworthy. It was patterned after a cod-fisherman's dory, fifteen feet long by three and a half feet wide, at its greatest breadth, and painted green with a border of blue, as Henry said "with reference to the two elements in which it was to spend its existence."

The evening before they had loaded the boat at their home, half a mile from the river, with home-grown potatoes and melons, cooking utensils, a tent of cotton cloth, and a buffalo skin, to be their bed. They had provided wheels to roll the boat around waterfalls, two sets of oars, and poles for shoving in shallow places, also two masts, one of which was to hold up their tent at night.

Henry concealed the disturbed state of his heart from his Journal and, presumably, from John. He had been the loser in the earnest contest for Ellen's smiles, and John would certainly be thinking of her all the while—so would he. But did they talk of her? When two young men, vigorously in love with a charming girl, set out in close confinement in a small boat, what was likely to happen? A sullen withdrawal into their shells? Jealous recriminations? Boasting? Accusations? Increasing strain? Blows?

No one knows. There was no peephole in the curtain of words which Henry set down six years later in his book about the trip. Possibly the brothers realized that the subject was too dangerous to broach at the time and perhaps too painful afterward. It is likely that each young man may have determined to make the best of the trip they had so long anticipated with pleasure. And they had been lifelong friends. Yet in that book John is not referred to by name, nor is he allowed to say one word. The heart of none is wholly searchable.

Henry, fortunately, had recourse to a more dependable love, his infatuation with the myriad aspects of nature. When he came to write the book, he humorously magnified the tone of his report. The voyagers "weighed anchor," like Captain Cook starting to sail around the globe. The launching place was termed a "river port," the flags and bulrushes "curtseyed a God-speed," some village friends "stood upon a promontory to wave a last farewell," and, as befits the departure of a flagship for some distant continent, they got out their guns and fired a farewell salute. It is a wonder Henry did not call them cannon. In a moment, the two brothers were floating past "the first regular battle ground of the Revolution." Henry wrote "regular" to distinguish Concord's fight from the earlier shots exchanged at Lexington.

By the time they had put the village sounds behind them and reached the Great Meadows, Henry's eyes, if not his heart, were busy with nature again—a pickerel driven from the covert of the lily pads, a bream frightened from her nest, the tortoises dropping into the water as the *Musketaquid* approached, the hibiscus flowers illuminating the dwarf willows. The last Concordian seen was a man on the bank fishing with a long birch pole, its silvery bark left on, a dog at his side. He reminded Henry of other fishermen, especially an old codger, "a straight old man he was who took his way in silence through the meadows, having passed the period of communication with his fellows; his old experienced coat hanging long and straight and brown as the yellow pine bark, glittering with so much smothered sunlight."

Nature did more than offer spectacles to Henry Thoreau; it helped him lift his reporting into poetry, which is a kind of condensation—"*experienced* coat, *smothered* sunlight." He liked to carry what he saw in his mind until it mellowed into philosophy, as here, where he fancied the old man's fishing not a sport, nor solely a means of subsistence, "but a sort of solemn sacrament and withdrawal from the world, just as the aged read their Bibles."

Even with both young men rowing, seven miles seemed far enough that Saturday afternoon, so they moored the *Musketaquid* near a huckleberry patch, pitched the tent, kindled a fire, and, for once, had no baked beans for supper. They made a meal of bread, cocoa, sugar, and berries, with no trace of human life to mar the wildness which Henry was always coveting. His sleep was spasmodically broken by foxes stepping about over the dead leaves. A musquash's fumbling along the potatoes and melons in the boat woke both campers. They ran sleepily to the stream but "could

81

detect only a ripple in the water ruffling the disk of a star."
Thus Henry made poetry of inconvenience.

What with owls hooting, sparrows bickering, house dogs
barking afar, and finally roosters crowing, the voyagers had
little sleep. Sunday's dawn brought fog, but quiet, and the
river was a perfect mirror to shave by. "The stillness was
intense and almost conscious, as if it were a natural Sabbath"
and Henry felt at home, for any place destitute of human
beings was home to him, so recently released from noisy
Cambridge and the very small talk of the Mill Dam. He
thought, "There is in my nature, a singular yearning toward
all wildness. I know of no redeeming quality in myself but
a sincere love for some things, and when I am reproved
I fall back on this ground."

Concord village was not shown this streak of humility, and
no public utterance by Henry had as yet disclosed this other
side of the sticky young man. Fortunately, he had this fathom-
less reservoir of peace within his reach. The vast untamed
reaches of nature became his sanctuary from mortal turmoil,
and he loved earth and sky so deeply that they were his
assurance of immortal good forever. On that morning of
utter quiet, he remembered that "on this same stream a
maiden once sailed in my boat, thus unattended but by
invisible guardians, and as she sat in the prow there was
nothing but herself between the steersman and the sky."

If poetry is emotion remembered in tranquillity, Henry
was easing his jealousy through the peace of the river. John
was certainly thinking of Ellen Sewall, too, and so that
morning there were four persons, so to speak, in the boat
without overcrowding it.

Henry had recovered his humor by the time they had passed "ancient Billerica, now in its dotage. I never heard that it was young." They passed the road to Carlisle which "gets laughed at because it is a small town." But Henry admits that great men may be born there any day, and the winds do not mind blowing over it. Jests were the ballast of Henry's being and kept his mentality balanced.

But imagination was his mentality's motive power. He now tried to think back to the white man's coming to this region, and seeming to the Indians "pale as the dawn, with a load of thoughts, with a slumbering intelligence as a fire raked up." He makes the imaginative suggestion that "this is New Angle-land, and these are the new West Saxons, whom the red men call, not Angle-ish or English, but Yengeese, and so at last they are known as Yankees." Have historians a sounder explanation for the name?

By now Henry may have recovered from his low state to realize that he did possess a few redeeming qualities after all —vigor, skill with his hands, enthusiasms ranging from nature to Homer, a thirst for books, an ear for music, a pulse for poetry, a heart for friendship, an eye for birds, another eye for men's follies, a sense of the comic, a zest for telling the world what was wrong for it and then offering a short cut to sure happiness.

He was hardly tactful, but he was honest. Indeed, he was integrity personified, a character clear-cut at twenty-two. In Concord village he was thought a queer duck, but Henry could call names, too, and more picturesquely than the Mill Damites. For him, culture must be accompanied by character to have force. And in a remark to John he focused his disdain for lack of character by speaking of a highly cultivated neighbor "all whose bones can be bent."

The *Musketaquid* passed Chelmsford, and John had been old enough when the Thoreaus lived there to remember some prophetic aspects of his brother, who was afraid of nothing. When Henry stooped to pat some new chicks, the mother hen swooped at him and knocked him down; but he did not cry. The infant naturalist embraced any stray dog or famished cat, but the animals felt his affection and neither bit nor scratched. "But you weren't very good at geography," John might have reminded him. "After getting a medal for excellence from that school in Boston, you could still ask, 'Mother, is Boston in Concord?'"

To reach the Merrimack River, the brothers towed their boat by hand through the Middlesex Canal. Even though it was the day of rest, they persuaded the lock-keeper to let them through the locks and down into the river. Henry, remembering his Sabbath imprisonments, exulted in his heathen freedom.

The Merrimack's waters, born of the White Mountains, and pouring down the mile-high slopes of Mount Washington, drained countless ravines and valleys. Henry pictured the river as the "key" which unlocked the whole geographical maze and put the outflow of water into a natural order.

Rowing against such a torrent was strenuous, but the athletes, as John and Henry really were, met the physical difficulties with good humor, and objected only to the man-made obstructions, such as dams and Manchester's mills. In the evenings, with the boat drawn up on some unfrequented bank, the tent erected, supper eaten, and the fire dreamily talking to itself, the voyagers traded ideas and humors.

What do young men talk about in such relaxed situations? The morrow's weather, the new aspects of the countryside, their occupations and hopes, their friends, their girls, and as darkness falls and confidences come more easily, they may discuss temptations and morals and religion.

Since John and Henry were both school teachers, both inhabitants of a tight little community rich in extraordinary characters, both full of hopes and prospects that needed fuller expression, they probably talked late, if not always in the most comfortable circumstances. Henry describes one evening of rain: "the drops come trickling down the stubble while we lie drenched on a bed of withered oats, by the side of a bushy hill, and the gathering in of the clouds, with the last rush and dying breath of the wind, and then the regular dripping of twigs and leaves the country over enhance the sense of inward comfort and sociableness."

The drenching must have come before they had put up the tent, and one wonders at no mention of a fire. But discomfort never impeded Henry's flow of thoughts. He particularly liked to air his views on books and poetry, and thought it a hearty recommendation when the book could stand the test of unobstructed sunshine. "What would we not give for some great poems to read now, which would be in harmony with the scenery!" he exclaimed. He considered poetry a natural fruit. "As naturally as the oak bears an acorn, the vine a gourd, man bears a poem, either spoken or done." His Indians tended to prove this novel idea true: they spoke in metaphor. But Henry adds, "Man is the great poet, and not Homer or Shakespeare; our language itself, and the common arts of life are his work."

The young teacher had slowly developed into a thinker who carried his thinking a step farther than the customary and so became original. His thinking was all the more sound for being done away from his desk. His manual actions got into his blood and bore their rhythms into his brain and mind. He recommended such activity as a sound preparation for writing. "The scholar may be sure that he writes the tougher truth for the callouses on his palms."

Emerson was going to contradict this dictum and lay down the rule that the scholar should not dig. But Henry contended that "a sentence should read as if its author, had he held a plow instead of a pen, could have drawn a furrow deep and straight to the end." Even John, who took life more easily than his brother, agreed when Henry said, "The truly efficient laborer will not crowd his day with work, but will saunter to his task surrounded by a wide halo of ease and leisure, and then do but what he loves best."

This coupling of labor and leisure, of maintaining one's individuality in choosing one's activities, was to become Henry Thoreau's guide to happy living. Not business before pleasure, the old Puritan maxim, but business with pleasure, or business *the* pleasure itself. "Let a man take time enough for the most trivial deed, though it be but the paring of his nails. The buds swell imperceptibly, without hurry or confusion, as if the short spring days were an eternity."

Henry wisely reinforced his argument with some hammer blow, some observation of nature, on the precept to be driven in. He said, "Though the hen should sit all day, she could lay only one egg, and besides, would not have picked up materials for another." John might have argued that man is more than a hen, or even a spring bud, but, had he been a writer, he would have recognized the advisability of following the hen's example.

As the trip progressed, Henry was enjoying some of the rewards of the effort taken: the discovery of new and beautiful country, the companionship with John, even though John was likely thinking of Ellen much of the time. Henry was also warming his heart with moods that went deeper than enjoyment, even as deep as religion, as he thought of religion without benefit of clergy. It was wonderful to find the "universe in such capital health. I think undoubtedly it will never die. Heal yourselves, doctors; by God I live.

> Then idle Time ran gadding by
> And left me with Eternity alone.

I see, smell, taste, hear, feel that everlasting Something to which we are allied, at once our maker, our abode, our destiny, our very selves; the one historic truth, the most remarkable fact which can become the distinct and uninvited subject of our thought, the actual glory of the universe; the only fact which a human being cannot avoid recognizing, or in some sense forget or dispense with."

The days were as full of circumstance as the evenings of talk and thoughts unspoken. The travelers were engrossed by the Amoskeag Falls at Manchester, though Henry regretted that they had been enslaved for the commercial purpose of turning water wheels. They hailed the hardy lumbermen herding flotillas of logs downstream, and again Henry mourned that whole forests were being felled for utilitarian purposes. He was becoming America's Number One Conservationist. He and John saluted the brawny New Hampshire fellows steering canalboats down the river, and Henry envied their rude heath, and, uncharacteristically, voiced no criticism of their equally rude language.

At length the Merrimack narrowed and flowed with such force that it became too strong to combat. The voyagers tied up their boat and became explorers on foot. Nor did they stop until they stood atop New Hampshire's Mount Washington. They loved the climbing and the wildness, and Henry extolled his ideal of land travel: "carrying a dipper, a spoon and a fish-line, some Indian meal, some salt and some sugar." He added, "I have traveled thus some hundreds of miles without taking any meal in a house, sleeping on the ground when convenient, and found it cheaper, and in many respects more profitable than staying at home." Then he delivered his usual jab at the lazy by saying he did not mean "travel sitting, the sedentary travelers whose legs hang dangling the while, but I mean those to whom traveling is life for the legs."

The two school teachers on vacation still attracted children, at times to the point of discipleship. Once when John sought to buy a loaf of bread at a farmhouse, he returned with a keen towheaded boy, who brought, as Henry put it, "some tradition, or small edition, of Robinson Crusoe in his head." He had listened to John telling his father of the voyage and wanted to join the brothers. They would have liked to take him with them, "but Nathan was still his father's boy, and had not come to years of discretion."

The two wits played one small joke when they were entertained in New Hampshire's Concord. They persisted in calling the town *New* Concord, since their own Concord was two centuries older. Henry does not mention how their condescension was received.

It speaks well for the country morals of that day that on returning to the Merrimack River, the voyagers found the *Musketaquid* as they had left it, with stores intact. But they learned that even New Hampshire folk could steal melons. One farmer took John and Henry to see his melon patch and revealed his method of dissuading thieves. He had stretched a rope around the patch a foot above the ground and connected it with a shotgun pointed along the line. On pleasant nights, the farmer sat in a shelter nearby as an added defense against thieves. The brothers sympathized with the farmer's human, if not humane, interest in protecting his property. Henry's sympathy with this cold-blooded arrangement reveals a side of him that may surprise his admirers.

The voyagers lugged a huge melon back to the river and set it to cool among some alders at the mouth of a creek, but it got away from them while they were pitching the tent and had to be pursued.

When they awoke the next morning, they "heard the faint deliberate and ominous sound of rain drops on our cotton roof," and the chill air announced that autumn had arrived. Since the wind was blowing downstream, they kept the sail set and, with the current to help, made good time.

"We endeavored in vain to persuade the wind to blow through the long corridor of the canal," Henry wrote, and so had to pull the boat. Nor were wind and current in their favor as they headed up the Concord River. Yet on the last day they made fifty miles, and "leaped gladly on shore, drawing up the boat and fastening it to the wild apple tree, whose stem still bore the mark which the chain had worn in the chafing of the spring freshets."

When the brothers finally trudged home to enjoy Cynthia's feast of welcome and relate what had happened, their story could have been short. They had suffered no great hardships nor molestations. The countryside, apart from the White Mountains, was unspectacular. The weather had been unexceptional for the first fortnight of September. What they had talked about was their own affair. The most troublesome English teacher who ever assigned a composition would not have asked a student to write a *book* about so modest and unstirring a trip.

Yet when Henry set himself this task six years later, he produced a volume of 518 pages, 200 of which concerned the river journeying—the week afoot was omitted—and the rest a report on his intellectual interests. These little essays ranged from discussions of Chaucer and Sir Walter Raleigh's literary style to the nature and function of poetry; from local history to the theory of deserts; from the character of time to the effects of music on the soul and the ways of friendship, with asides on the Huguenots on Staten Island and Neoplatonism and the Pythagoreans.

Thus one observes how a few acorns become a forest. But before Henry wrote *A Week on the Concord and Merrimack*

Rivers, the stream of his own life began to run faster, with threatening rapids and whirlpools which racked his spirit to the point of heartbreak. It was for John's sake that he would tell the story of their halcyon voyage and instill in it the fairest parable of friendship that his torn heart could form.

SIX

A Love, a Death, and a Decision

HOW good it was to be home—that first evening. But the two weeks of freedom from the incessant chatter of that home revealed to Henry that he must find some shelter from it. How could he escape the perpetual intrusion on his thoughts? How was he to concentrate on his true work, the sizing-up of life?

As he was turning over the pages of his Journal, he noticed his first entry, "I seek a garret." That was the answer. The little upper room of yellow-washed boards at the top of the house would do. In a few days, this was transformed into a satisfactory retreat. Shelves housed his books and notebooks, the arrowheads and curious stones he had carried home. The walls were hung with cocoons, seed pods, and other booty of his rambles. No voices from downstairs penetrated, and best of all, he could hear the rains beat on the roof.

Yet, even in his cherished solitude, Henry was not easy. John had hurried off to Scituate and Ellen, spent two nights there and walked on the dunes with her. Henry could only release his emotions in poetry:

A LOVE, A DEATH, AND A DECISION

I think a while of love, and while I think,
    Love is to me a world,
    Sole meat and sweetest drink,
    And close connecting link
'Tween heaven and earth.
I only know it is, not how or why,
    My greatest happiness;
    However hard I try,
    Not if I were to die,
    Can I explain.

I fain would ask my friend how it can be,
    But when the time arrives,
    Then love is more lovely
    Than anything to see,
    And so I'm dumb.

On John's return he was equally silent, and Henry had to turn to other company. Thanks to Mr. Emerson, he had plenty.

In Henry's copy of *Hamlet,* it would not be surprising to find these lines underscored: "There's a divinity that shapes our ends, / Rough-hew them how we will." For Henry must have been conscious that, whenever he seemed to be face to face with a blank wall, a door opened before him. Again and again throughout his life, Ralph Waldo Emerson appeared to be the agent appointed by Divinity to open the door.

Women, it is true, often had a hand on the doorknob. In this case, it was Mrs. Lucy Jackson Brown, the sister of Emerson's wife, who set it ajar. She was still boarding at

93

the Thoreau home. One day, she returned from hearing a lecture of Emerson's so full of his fine thoughts that she began quoting them to Helen Thoreau.

"Why, you might suppose he had got them from Henry!" Helen exclaimed, and both women laughed at this bold idea.

"Seriously, though," Helen went on, "I have read those very thoughts and opinions in my brother's Journal."

"Mercy!" cried Lucy Brown. "Does he permit you to read his precious Journal? I thought journals were the hiding places of confidences too intimate to be divulged."

"Henry doesn't mind. Wait, I'll show you." So Helen ran upstairs, with some loss of breath, found the parallel passages, and read them to Mrs. Brown. The latter was so impressed that the next time she saw Emerson, she informed him of his rival thinker.

Emerson was a generous man and expressed a desire to talk with this like-minded youth. They had met on the street and yet had had no real conversation. Emerson's social circle did not include the Thoreaus. Also, the author of *Nature* and *The American Scholar* was busy writing lectures for the Lyceum and helping Margaret Fuller publish a new magazine for learned circles called *The Dial*. In addition, he found time to conduct conversations at his capacious home on Lexington Road. Boston abounded in talkers and they sought Emerson's hospitable parlor as confidently as water seeks its own level.

After being so stirred by *Nature,* Henry had been curious about these discussions behind the closed shutters of Emerson's intellectual castle. Orestes Brownson had shown Henry what talk could be. Every nugget-like phrase in Emerson's writings had whetted the young man's interest in this nature-praiser. But the older man was reputed to be cold and Henry could be equally reticent. So he felt both curious and challenged as he approached his first extended exchange with his now famous neighbor.

What did he see as Emerson opened the door? A tallish man in his thirties, with fine brown hair, a broad forehead, a mouth ready to smile, and blue eyes whose glance seemed to penetrate to Henry's heart and mind. His voice was welcoming, for he loved youth and desired to help the aspiring. When young Thoreau stood before him, sturdy, ruddy from the sun, with deep-set eyes fearless and searching, Emerson was startled. Here was a stanch countryman with a spirit obviously as erect in mind as in body. It was almost like finding the spiritual man he had long visualized.

That was an important meeting and both men sensed its value.

"We first met when I was nine," Henry said. "I sang in the choir of the fiftieth anniversary of the Battle."

Emerson knew that Henry was referring to the lines he had written for that occasion, beginning, "By the rude bridge that arched the flood." "Come in and meet some fellow thinkers," he said. "You will provide fresh air from your walks and reflections. I think you have met my wife Lidian."

Henry had indeed met the gracious lady and looked forward to a closer acquaintance with her. Now he was taken into the parlor and introduced to two men and a woman who were to become lifelong friends: William Ellery Channing, a nephew of Henry's Harvard professor, an enthusiastic walker who was to become Henry's most frequent companion; Bronson Alcott, the genial, unpractical philosopher, serene as the blue sky, and just about as useful in down-to-earth matters; and Margaret Fuller, the sister of Channing's wife, a plain intellectual, whose mind soared so far into the air that it might be termed flighty. Lidian Emerson, the shy, the considerate, often amused observer of her husband's friends, made the newcomer feel at home.

Common-sense Henry, as can be guessed, was at first rather mystified by the conversation, especially when other intellectuals arrived from Boston and inflated the talk with their rather unpractical ideas. They were hoping to improve the world at once. They were scholars versed in the writings of European philosophers and were forever quoting intellectual formulas for the better life from authors Henry had not encountered, even in the Harvard Library. Their learning shamed him, but the uses to which they put it seemed too airy and unsubstantial to interest him. He thought these earnest thinkers very funny because their talk tended to vaporize amid the starry spaces. They called themselves Transcendentalists who longed to experience life to its farthest bounds. Their favorite subject was "the universe." They led Henry to make a famous remark, later, about cloud castles in the air, "That is where they should be; now put the foundations under them." He was also to say, "One piece of good sense would be more memorable than a monument as high as the moon."

Actually, Henry liked his own thought to soar in the high heavens, but chiefly that it might return with some superior truth. Funny or not, this gathering provided the most satisfying atmosphere, *inside* a house, that Henry had sat in yet. He became a fairly regular visitor at Emerson's home. He appreciated Lidian Emerson's wise gentleness. He had heard so much about her from her sister at his own table that he already felt quietly acquainted.

Nor was the appreciation one-sided. Emerson was soon writing in *his* Journal—everybody kept journals—"My good Henry Thoreau made this else solitary afternoon sunny with his simplicity and clear perception. How comic is simplicity in this double-dealing, quacking world. Everything that boy says makes merry with society, though nothing can be graver than his meaning. I told him he should write out the history of his college life."

This Henry, characteristically, did *not* do. He did not like to be "told." Although he was "that boy" to Emerson (and Henry was only twenty-one), he felt that he had found his footing and he did not intend to kowtow to his host and helper.

"What do you propose to do with your scholarship?" Emerson asked one day when the two were alone.

Henry acknowledged that he would rather raise melons and saunter in the wilds than assist the Transcendentalists in founding any new society. It was becoming clear to the young man that people's aims were unsteady because their ends were unsure. His own ambition was fixed: *to mind his own business and endeavor to be what he was made to be.*

So far, so good. But how to accomplish this successfully when everyone advocated that he apply himself more purposefully? That was the question.

As his visits to the Lexington Road home continued,

Henry found it strange how little *fact* Emerson knew about
that nature which was his first great subject. Emerson's
"nature" was literary, philosophical, ideal; while Henry
brought the seer's eyes down to earth and made him *see* the
world of lichens, mayflies, Indian pots.

He was so apt at finding the red men's relics that Emerson
said, "They spring out of the ground and arrange themselves
in Henry's path when he wishes to reveal Indian history to
me."

Emerson had written, "The foregoing generations beheld
God and nature face to face; we, through their eyes. Why
should not we enjoy an original relation to the universe?"
And here was the answer to his question, walking beside him
on the trail to Walden Pond—a youth with a nose made to
point the way, and eyes to verify what the nose announced.
By now, Henry knew the countryside like a fox or the birds,
and he lived in precisely that original relation to nature which
Emerson advocated.

Fame had not made Emerson less generous and quick in
his admirations. Soon he was talking of Henry as *"the* man"
of Concord. Henry must have smiled at the village's amazement at this news. And any of his Harvard classmates who
heard this pronouncement must have doubted their ears. If
young Thoreau had been made of easier fiber and less resolute
in his aim "to be what he was made," he might have adjusted,
little by little, to meet Emerson's views, and so have become
less and less himself. Praise has its dangers, and this was one
of the dangerous periods in Henry's danger-filled life. Yet he
remained stoutly the sturdy, determined, truth-seeking, free-
dom-loving youth he had been. He saw clearly, as he wrote

later, "What a man thinks of himself, that it is which determines, or rather indicates, his fate."

During the December vacation of their school, Prudence Ward took John and Henry to visit the Sewalls by the sea. It was not a happy occasion for Henry—he had too much time alone. He expressed his mood in a beautiful poem, "The Fisher's Son," and on returning to Concord, he sent some of his verses to Ellen. She forgot to acknowledge them. But John, always more experienced with girls, sent her opals for her collection of minerals, with a letter. Ellen thanked *him*, and said she had read his letter to her young brother "again and again." Henry had not helped matters by suggesting to Ellen that she stop drinking tea and coffee for clear thinking's sake! Our novice had not yet realized that any effort to convert womankind to anything implied that they could be improved, which was insulting!

In June of the following year, 1840, Ellen visited Concord again, and again permitted Henry to row her around. But it was John who returned to the sea, with the Wards, walked with the lovely girl on the beach and proposed marriage. Out of joy or inexperience, the eighteen-year-old Ellen said *Yes.*

Meanwhile, Henry was steeped in gloom at the girl's obvious preference for his brother and wrote in his Journal, "July 19, 1840. These two days that I have not written in my Journal, set down in the calendar as the 17th and 18th of July, have been really an aeon in which a Syrian empire might rise and fall."

When John returned, uplifted by Ellen's acceptance of him, the blow to Henry was devastating. But soon it was

John's turn to suffer: Ellen allowed herself to be persuaded by her parents that the marriage could not take place. They thought that the Thoreaus, with their free-thinking minds and boarding-house lives, were distinctly below the Sewall standard.

The romantic seesaw quickly lifted Henry into the seventh heaven and, on August 7, he wrote in his Journal, "A wave of happiness flows over me like moonshine over a field."

It was, alas, merely moonshine. Neither document nor supposition remains to reveal the *reason* in Henry's actions during these tides of sentiment. Did John disclose to him the Sewalls' prejudices which resulted in the broken engagement? If so, did Henry conclude that he could override them? Ellen had been sent off to her uncle's family in Watertown, New York, and Henry corresponded. Since distance made it impossible for him to go to her during the school session, and since he could not bear to wait, he offered marriage by letter.

Biographers gag at this impulsive passion on the part of the usually cool and critical Henry Thoreau. They cannot believe that the youth could be so unpredictably in love, or act in such illogical haste. Why should a girl, who had always shown her preference for John, accept his postal offer? Did he *wish* to be refused for some psychological reason, unclear even to himself? Or was he simply an inexperienced boy, swept off his feet by vivid imaginings of his happiness with Ellen?

He haunted the post office for another Scythian aeon. Finally, on November 10, Ellen wrote her refusal "in a short explicit and cold manner," as her father had demanded.

A LOVE, A DEATH, AND A DECISION

So Henry had to fall back on philosophy, his own and Emerson's. "Man's life is a progress, not a station," was one of these exhortations to the brave who are temporarily disappointed. But Henry had also schoolteaching to divert his thoughts. In addition, he and John had been drawn closer than ever now, in their common misfortune. John's health was shaky. The gay young schoolmaster, who could induce an unruly boy to change his ways by a word or a pat on the shoulder, was unable to rid himself of his cough. The Thoreau household worried at his increasing pallor.

Henry tried to lessen his brother's fatigue by taking over some of his duties, but that was not enough. A protracted spell of illness indicated that the invalid must have a change of climate. But what of the school? Henry considered hiring a substitute, yet knew in his heart that there could be no second John. Better close the school than putter along with an inferior assistant. Besides, another question troubled Henry. Did he wish to continue teaching for the rest of his days?

John's illness, Henry's barely healed heartbreak over Ellen, this new shattering indecision, darkened the days. There is no record of the Thoreau family's feelings when Henry determined to close the school. But when he announced to the assembled boys and girls that they must seek their schooling elsewhere, a quiet, as if a death had occurred, settled on the room. The least studious of the youngsters could understand that there would be no more outdoor excursions, no more laughing with John or shrieks of pretended affront at Henry's puns. Instead, they would return to threats and thrashings and dull learning of dates and battles by rote.

After the first shock, boys as well as girls asked what they could do for John. Were there errands to run? Woodboxes to fill? Henry informed them that John was to be moved to his mother's people at Bridgewater, south of Boston, nearer the healthful influence of the sea.

Young Horace Hosmer asked Henry what he would do— "just walk in the woods?"

"I could do worse, Horace. Nobody yet has succeeded in bringing a star indoors."

Henry's thought leaped to Walden Pond and White Pond, whose waters could fetch you a star down from the sky. He wondered what other occupation could give you the short hours and the long vacations of schoolkeeping. He could buy a farm and eke out a living on it. Concord's climate offered a farmer long winters in which to ruminate. He had eyed the Hallowell Farm for some time. It was in a sufficiently ruinous condition to come cheap and engage his energies outdoors where he belonged. Yet some ancestral cautions held him back from actual outlay of cash. In his Journal, on March 27, 1841, he wrote, "I must not lose any of my freedom by being a farmer and landholder. Most who enter on any profession are doomed men. The world might as well sing a dirge over them forthwith."

Yet he *had* to do something to help with John's doctor's bills. He was now twenty-four and must be able to answer Horace Hosmer's question, which others were asking, too. He himself was sure of the answer. His desire, his necessity, his duty was to *be*. He had reached one fixed decision: not to be a slave. He would choose the sort of earning a living that left him some life to live, or at least crippled his freedom the least. He determined to keep his whole day as fresh as its morning. Outdoors, every morning invited him to live cheerfully with equal simplicity. You couldn't get away from that thought, *simplicity*. And how did you achieve a state of simplicity? By simplifying your life.

The superficial observer is defeated by Henry at this troubled stage of his life and finds him utterly selfish, callous, intent solely on his happiness. His family knew him better. He helped in all the daily duties, from taking the cow to pasture after the morning milking to shooing the chickens into their house at nightfall. He tended garden, ran errands for the boarders, and did chores for the neighbors to bring in ready money. There were chimneys to clean, fences to be mended, and, most tedious of all, assisting his father at pencil making—*and* selling.

His occupations, plus his observations of the merchants on the Mill Dam, the farmers, mechanics, and others half drowned in the stream of commerce, all tended to convince him that this busyness was overdone. His neighbors were smothering their real selves by devoting all of their time to "getting ahead," as they called it. Ahead of what? Aunt Maria was forever quoting Isaac Watts, "For Satan finds some mischief still for idle hands to do." Henry chuckled at his reply to his unimaginative aunt, "Isaac Watts has done more mischief by that remark than Satan could accomplish in years. "

One thing was certain: he refused to wither up before his time. He was going to order his life, and not have it ordered by someone else. He would live it so as to get the most possible life out of it, as *he* understood life, and *out of each day*

103

as it came. People celebrated the nation's Independence Day but neglected to secure one of their own.

Henry's critics who condemned him as lazy, as self-centered and selfish, either had forgotten the days of their youth, when the whole course of life had to be determined, or had never had the spunk to care. True, he always came back to himself in his thoughts, but what youth doesn't, or shouldn't? It was becoming clearer to him with every day that was swallowed up in chartless activity that he must discover his vocation beyond any possibility of self-deception. He had had inklings of this calling, but the need of dollars got in his way. How could he earn and at the same time live fully? What youth has not been confronted with the same question?

At length the doctor felt it safe for John to return to Concord, and Henry welcomed the person who was dearest to him in all his world. John looked frail, in comparison with the happy days of their trip on the rivers, but his spirits were gay. No mention was made of the Sewall affair, which had threatened to estrange the two brothers. John told Henry of the new species of birds that had come to his feeding station at Bridgewater, and Henry, who was so reserved with others about matters close to his heart, talked over his problem of sustaining himself with his brother.

"My Journal has known all along, what I have been slow to understand," Henry said. "I must write."

"A writer must have something to say," John warned him.

"I have my days, my thoughts, reality, the truth. They are burden enough for a score of books."

A LOVE, A DEATH, AND A DECISION

"That's half of your problem solved," John said judiciously. "But will you have buyers? You have devoured *Nature*, and Mrs. Brown told Mother that Emerson is well known abroad as well as here. She also said that the sale was only five hundred copies. Subtract the costs from that return, and what have you? A deficit."

Henry's look roved about his garret, for his books and treasures helped to fortify his views of his destiny, and his features grew fixed to reflect the stubbornness within him. "Life keeps offering me freedom, John. I am a traitor to the best in me if I do not seize it."

"Freedom?" John stared into the clear blue eyes of his brother. Henry could be maddeningly incomprehensible. "What freedom?"

"Our school ends, and frees me. Ellen—frees me."

John quickly detoured around that subject and said, "Go to New York and be a newspaperman."

"Into slavery?" Henry cried fiercely. "And abdicate all I stand for? Never!" He felt half sick that his own brother could so misunderstand him. "The trouble is how to live *truly* while writing. If I can do that, the writing will be true." He opened a notebook on the table, turned a few pages and said, "I sewed up that dilemma in this couplet:

"My life has been a poem I would have writ,
But I could not both live and utter it."

John nodded in agreement. "That's it, of course," but he gazed at his brother in concern. Henry was so stubbornly true to himself, so narrowly true in the opinion of most, that he would not yield an inch—and sometimes that broke people.

Henry was saying, "That old fool Polonius uttered the final truth through his politician's lying lips, without meaning a word of it. 'To thine own self be true, / And it must follow, as the night the day, / Thou canst not then be false to any man.' And what follows then?" Henry looked at his brother questioningly.

"Why, I suppose they call you reliable."

"What does it matter what they call you?" Henry retorted. "*Then* you have got your bearings. You are headed right. You are walking even with the Builder of the Universe."

John was silenced. How could he remind his brother, in this exalted mood, that one had to have money? Yet, to be incorruptible as Henry was, was much. Indeed it was everything. John was almost ashamed that he had offered something less than Henry's integrity demanded. The talk turned to other matters.

Emerson's offer followed this talk so swiftly that, to John, it seemed as if Providence had overheard Henry—and approved.

The great man needed help himself. His stimulating lectures on *Heroism, Self-Reliance, Compensation, The Over-Soul,* had brought him invitations to appear on distant platforms. He hesitated to leave his wife and a houseful of young children without a man handy. Yet this man must be acceptable to Lidian, who was described by her husband as "too pensive, careful, and melancholy." She suggested Henry, and Emerson approved. He would offer young Thoreau the small room at the head of the stairs, his meals, and the use of his library, if he would do the chores and keep an eye on the children.

Henry felt obliged to accept. He liked outdoor jobs and had an easy way with children that attracted them to him. Also, he knew it would please Lucy Jackson Brown to have him look after Lidian, and Henry owed Mrs. Brown much. When he was three years younger, he had picked a bunch of violets, tied them together with a wisp of straw, added a poem, and tossed the bouquet through her open window. The poem was titled;

Sic Vita
I am a parcel of vain strivings tied
By a chance bond together,
Dangling this way and that, their links
Were made so loose and wide,
Methinks
For milder weather.

As a poem of feelings, it was mildness itself. But Mrs. Brown, several years older, was sympathetic and interested, and gave him a hearing. All the young man needed was to find his confidences welcomed; he supplied them. And some, a little too intimate for speech, were entrusted to his Journal, "I know a woman who is as true to me and as incessant with her mild rebuke as the blue sky. . . . Her eyes are such bottomless and inexhaustible depths as if they were the windows of the Nature, through which I caught glimpses of the native land of the soul."

When Mrs. Brown returned to her home in Plymouth, he wrote to her: "Dear Friend. . . . We always seem to be living just on the brink of a pure and lofty intercourse, which would make the ills and trivialities of life ridiculous. I seem to have dodged all my days with one or two persons, and lived upon expectations—as if the bud would surely blossom; and so I am content to live. . . . I am very happy in my present environment."

This environment was his new home with the Emerson family, with talk on a high plane, an atmosphere of cultivated quiet, and even affection. However, Henry saw little of Ralph Waldo Emerson, who was immured in his study, writing lectures or away delivering them. Lidian was there to consult on a score of matters, and the new household guardian spent long evenings in Emerson's fine library, poring over the books by religious writers of the 1600's. The great prose of the King James Version of the Bible got into his blood stream, as was happening to Abraham Lincoln on the far side of the Alleghenies, and floated him on its noble rhythms.

The eager youngsters did their mentor a good turn, too, and Edward—who was Eddy to all—later wrote of Henry in this long, picture-making sentence:

In childhood I had a friend—not a house friend, domestic, stuffy in association; nor yet herdsman, or horseman, or farmer, or slave of bench, of shop, or office; nor of letters, nor art, nor society; but a free, friendly, youthful-seeming man, who wandered in from unknown woods or fields without knocking—

"Between the night and day
When the fairy kind has power"

as the ballad says, passed by the elders' doors, but straightway sought out the children, brightened up the wood-fire forthwith; and it seemed as if it were the effect of a wholesome brave north wind, more than of the armful of "catsticks" which he would bring in from the yard. His type was Northern—strong features, light brown hair, an open-air complexion with suggestions of a seafaring race; the mouth pleasant and flexible when he spoke, aquiline nose, deep-set but very wide-open eyes of a clear blue gray, since but capable of a twinkle, and again of austerity, but not of softness. These eyes could not be made to rest on what was unworthy, saw much and keenly (but yet in certain directions hardy at all), and did not fear the face of clay. A figure short and narrow, but thick; a carriage assuring of sturdy strength and endurance. When he walked to get over the ground one thought of a tireless machine, seeing his long, direct, uniform pace; but his body was active and well balanced, and his step could be light, as of one who could leap or dance or skate well at will. His dress was strong and plain.

Henry's true nature emerged from behind his reserve when called out by the affection of sympathetic womanhood and loving youngsters. He could be a cut-up in the company of the Emerson tribe and the children of Bronson Alcott, who lived a little farther along the Lexington Road. He made pencils and knives vanish and then reappear from the ears of the enchanted girls and boys. He taught them how to name the birds, brought turtles for their pens, and tadpoles for the aquarium. At twenty-four, he was full of high spirits, a mimic, a bird-caller who could summon the crows about him—the Pied Piper of Concord village.

Henry initiated his youthful followers into the delights of roving through the deep woods. Curiously, the families of Concord, who went on temperance picnics, fished, picked berries, and gathered roadside flowers, left the woods largely alone. The exceptions were Henry's ne'er-do-wells, such as One-eyed Goodwin. So Henry led his tribe into the fairy-tale dimness, taught them woods lore, and they in turned loved their tamed bear. Henry could be brusque with his elders, but the broad strain of youth that persisted in him throughout his life echoed to their laughter and joyous shouts. With them, he could forget the problems which this congenial interlude had done little to solve.

All this while, however, Henry was confiding himself to his Journal, doubts and all: "I cannot tell you what I am, more than a ray of the summer's sun. What I am I am, and say not. Being is the great explainer. In the attempt to explain, shall I plane away all the spines, till it is no thistle, but a cornstalk?"

Henry was not averse to being a thistle, and prickly if touched in the wrong place. At home, frankness of opinion was accepted. Cynthia spoke what she thought, right out, nor did the aunts lag in candor. By contrast, the extreme politeness of the Emerson family irritated Henry. It seemed scarcely honest to conceal one's feelings. Presently, Henry discovered that Emerson would hold him at arm's length, however long he stayed. The great man admitted that he was cool, even remote. This was the usual complaint about Henry; but now the shoe was on the other foot—and pinched.

It irked Henry to be so near heaven's gate—the priceless opportunity for discussion—and never be invited in. He was bursting with thoughts, views, tendencies, objections, and contentions, and yearned for endless debate on the tremendous things in his mind. But Emerson pronounced, like a sovereign. He declined to be argued with. He was unskilled in descending from his own mental and spiritual elevation. "Though I prize my friends, I cannot afford to talk with them and study their visions lest I lose my own," Emerson wrote in his Journal. So Henry's ardor for disputing was continually being chilled by the polite mask he met at mealtimes.

Consequently, he walked with Ellery Channing, who overflowed with conversation, and delighted to differ with Henry.

"What do you see in the man?" John asked Henry one evening when his brother had come home for a call. "His mind's as flighty as a chipmunk. He uses it instead of a tail."

"That's a poor comparison," Henry objected. "A chipmunk uses his tail to balance with; Channing uses his mind to unbalance me. He's a trifler with ideas and leaves fact aside as of no importance. When I complain, he says, a bit petulantly, 'I am universal; I have nothing to do with the particular and definite.' "

"Why waste time with him then?" John persisted.

"He *walks*, although he sticks to the road and I prefer going cross lots. Then he has much of classic literature in his head. It's somewhat like strolling with the Harvard Library. Also, he likes to laugh and make laugh. Yesterday he said that he keeps a dog for society, to stir up the air of the room when it becomes dead. He experiences awful solitudes."

Henry amused his mother by his account of Margaret Fuller, who spent as much time in Concord as in Boston. "She differs from anyone I have seen or dreamt of," he told Cynthia. "She out-soars the other Transcendentalists, if that seems possible. In one of her usual ecstasies she cried out that she accepted the universe, which was gracious of her. When Mr. Emerson passed this news on to Mr. Carlyle, he wrote back, 'Gad! She'd better!' Fortunately she believes in publishing what she calls 'the newness of youth,' which admits me."

Miss Fuller had rejected Henry's essay on Walter Raleigh, but printed his critical opinion of a Latin poet, Persius, in that learned publication, *The Dial*. One happy by-product of this piece was a letter of appreciation from an inhabitant of Worchester, Harrison G. O. Blake, who became a lifelong friend of Henry's.

The young Thoreau interested Margaret Fuller in spite of herself. He irritated her because he neglected the little attentions and compliments which mean so much to women, and especially women like Miss Fuller, who had been overlooked by other men. Also, he spoke his mind with disturbing candor. She referred to Henry as "the enemy," and complained that he was "a bare hill, unwarmed by spring." But she accepted his writings and allowed him to edit *The Dial* for one year, and so pushed him along into the career of his choice.

Bronze bust of Thoreau by Malvina Hoffman

Old Indian trail, Walden

Walden Pond, from the air

Thoreau's hut at
Walden—and map

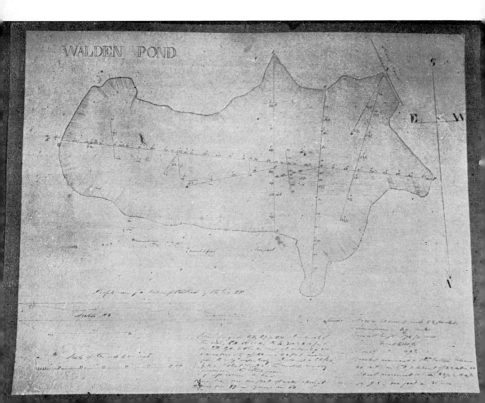

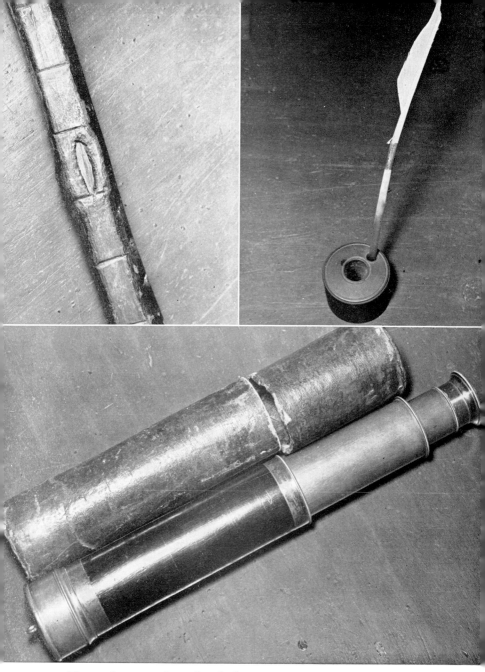

Thoreau's cane, inkstand and glass

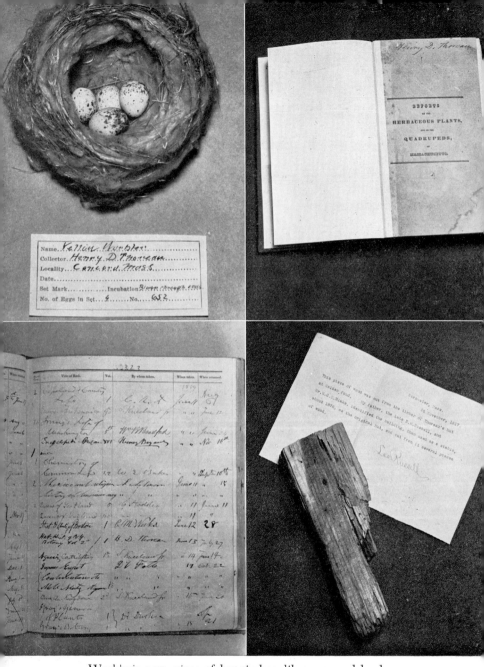

Warbler's nest, piece of hut-timber, library record book

Thoreau's grave

Walden Pond

A LOVE, A DEATH, AND A DECISION

Henry realized how fortunate he was in having such a stimulus in his country village. His accounts of Margaret Fuller in his Journal reveal how sharp an observer of persons he had become. He regrets that "our acquaintance plainly does not attain to that degree of confidence and sentiment which women, which all, in fact, covet," and adds, "Perhaps she does not make the highest demand on me, a religious demand. For a companion, I require one who will make an equal demand on me with my own genius. It is suicide, and corrupts good manners, to welcome any less than this. I value and trust those who love and praise my aspiration rather than my performance. If you would not stop to look at me, but look whither I am looking, and farther, then my education could not dispense with your company."

In those lines, clear as spring water, Henry had stated his idea of perfect, fruitful friendship. He was indeed expanding, like his river, thanks to the fresh influences which, as so many rivulets, had swelled and deepened his life.

Another continuing influence was Bronson Alcott, father of the lively Louisa May, whose book *Little Women* was one day to capture the world.

Alcott was a curious product of New England civilization, a practicing visionary. Henry called him "broad and genial, but indefinite; forever feeling about feebly in his speech and touching nothing." But he was sympathetic with Henry's most cherished fancy and erected no obstacles in the way of their meeting. "He has no creed," Henry wrote. "He is not pledged to any institution. The sanest man I ever knew; the fewest crotchets, after all has he. We walk together like the most innocent children, going after wild pinks with case-knives."

Alcott lived too high in the clouds to let his feet find earth. He tried schoolteaching in Boston, and instead of punishing unruly pupils, he smacked his own hand, in the hope that these sensitive little souls would be touched. They weren't. He held Conversations, at a small charge, but rambled on so interminably that people left. His loyal wife tried desperately to keep the family fed and clothed, and Emerson assisted. Yet Bronson Alcott must have been most helpful to Henry, by lending him a willing ear.

Miss Mary Moody Emerson, Ralph Waldo's aunt and adviser, lent both ears to Henry. She was that youthful egoist's idea of the perfect woman: witty, vivacious, the least frivolous, the most ready to listen while he uttered his best thought. "In short," as Henry told his brother John, "she is a genius, as woman seldom is, reminding you less often of her sex than any woman I know."

"No mirror could picture one side of you Henry, better than your praise of Aunt Mary Emerson," John said when his brother aired these views of his aged admirer—who was actually older than the United States. "One who does not know you would set you down as a conceited pup who likes women because they listen to him."

"It is a rare privilege to find such," Henry retorted.

"She scandalizes other women, you know. She has small respect for them and hushes them up when men are present. The other day, when Sophia was speaking of her flowers, Miss Emerson put a hand on her and said, 'Be still, I want to hear the men talk.'"

"Because we are more likely to have opinions of our own."

John laughed. "She has opinions! When Mother called on

her and was wearing that bonnet with the yellow ribbons, Aunt Mary kept her eyes closed until Mother rose to go. Then Aunt Mary rebuked her for such gaudy apparel as unbecoming to a woman her age."

"Even she!" Henry exclaimed. "So hard is it to put up with the slightest divergence of custom."

"Aunt Mary diverges, certainly—riding sidewise on a man's saddle, which even the tramps think unladylike, and wearing that scarlet shawl over the flannel shroud she has made for her funeral. Who is she to complain of yellow ribbons!"

"And you are still expecting consistency in people!"

"But wearing that shroud *already!*" John said. "In the name of conscience, why?"

"To save trouble, to be prepared, to be herself and therefore different. You heard what Mr. Emerson said about consistency last evening at the Lyceum: 'A foolish consistency is the hobgoblin of little minds, adored by little statesmen and philosophers and divines.' "

"I'm sure Aunt Mary would agree," John said, and the brothers laughed, little knowing that it was their last time for laughing together.

January, 1842, began with mild weather, and John had recovered from his illness sufficiently to walk outdoors. His list of birds seen in Concord was growing, and when he spotted an evening grosbeak, he scratched his hand rather deeply in climbing a fence to get closer to this rare specimen. The wound bled little, and John wrapped a rag about it and forgot it. In a day or so, it began to pain him. Cynthia soaked his hand, and when that failed to relieve the inflammation, poulticed it. Yet the ache spread from hand to arm and Dr. Bartlett was consulted. He lanced the swelling, saying, "There, by tomorrow you'll be feeling more comfortable." But on the morrow the pain began to pull at the arm like a bulldog. Dr. Bartlett, now alarmed, sent to Boston for a consultant. He pronounced the fateful word "lockjaw," and looked grave.

When Henry broke his news to Emerson, he cried out, "Oh! Oh! How are these things possible! Why, only the other day, John took Waldo to have his daguerreotype made. John is composed more of thoughtfulness than flesh. Henry, you must stay at home to help."

So Henry sat beside John through the frightening agony until kind death released the sufferer. So deeply was Henry sympathetic that his own body manifested some of John's symptoms. The days of prostrating grief buried something of Henry, too, in John's grave. His feeling for this gay and charming older brother, a lifelong affection, shadowed only by the rivalry for Ellen Sewall, now tortured him in this irreparable loss. He sought to relieve the ache as best he could by writing to his now dearest friend, Mrs. Lucy Brown, in words that omit so much of ordinary grief that they seem strange. "What right have I to grieve, who have not ceased to wonder?" At the ways of the universe, perhaps, for he was an apprenticed Transcendentalist, a believer in that philosophy which, according to Ralph Waldo Emerson, asserts the primacy of the spiritual and superindividual as against the material and what is based on experience. And Henry added,

A LOVE, A DEATH, AND A DECISION

"I do not wish to see John ever again—I mean him who is dead—but that other, whom only he would have wished to see, or to be, of whom he was the imperfect representative." A wish that the Reverend Ezra Ripley would have approved.

The letter went on, "For we treat or esteem each other for what we are capable of being"—which, as ever, was Henry's cry in times of intense feeling. The young man who had "signed off" church did so that he might worship God according to his own ideas, without an intermediary clergyman.

Two months after that barren January 11 of John's death, Henry cried out in his Journal, "My life, my life! why will you linger?" but went on, "Why, God, did you include me in your great scheme? Will you not make me a partner at last?"

This was the turning point in Henry's sorrow. It was not in his nature to resign himself long to events. He must resume his witnessing to creative Spirit. He returned to Emerson's home, to the memory-blunting routine of snow shoveling and firewood-cutting and the blessed atmosphere of children's gaiety.

Emerson's first-born child, Waldo, was Henry's particular pet. The boy was only five but already beamed with imagination and bubbled with fun. Henry loved him deeply and Waldo, feeling this, liked to be with his big brother in the garden or beside little Mill Brook, below the Emerson place, where the youngster tried to hold the water back with dams.

The woodshed was another happy place to visit, for Henry was whittling chips into creatures that Waldo knew—the animals which Adam had named and were destined for Noah's ark.

"What will you make for me today?" the child asked hopefully.

Henry pretended to think, then said, "Today, the king of beasts."

"What's a king?"

"He's the ruler. Remember the picture I showed you this morning?"

Waldo nodded. "The man with the funny thing on his head."

"Yes, but don't you let a king hear you say that."

Waldo laughed at the tone of Henry's voice. "I will; I'll say it to the first king I see."

Henry continued shaping the lion and Waldo asked, "Does the king of beasts have to wear the funny thing?"

"Did you ever see Puss wear one?"

Waldo shook his head. This conversation was not telling him much. But then Henry was a grownup part of the time. Waldo paid no attention to grownups as such. So Henry explained, "Animals know better than to dress up or wear crowns. There!" He held up the lion. "That's Puss's great big brother, lion."

"I know," Waldo said emphatically. "I saw him at that place where Papa took me." Waldo's father had walked with his son to see the traveling circus, and the boy had loved everything but the clown whose caricature of a man frightened him.

Emerson was particularly attached to this son who mirrored his own affectionate nature and shared his gift of fancy. Consequently, when the child came down with a slight fever, Ralph and Lidian Emerson worried but they were not unduly alarmed. They did not connect his illness with the scarlet fever which was seeking out victims in Concord that winter. Then, suddenly, the boy grew worse and died on January 27.

This death was all leaden loss, and for Henry, burdened to the point of torment by grief for John, it was overwhelming. Again he turned to Mrs. Lucy Brown and wrote that Waldo died "as the mist rises from the brook, which the sun will soon dart his rays through. Do not the flowers die every season? He had not even taken root here. I was not startled to hear that he was dead; it seemed the most natural death that could happen. His fine organization demanded it, and Nature gently yielded its request."

Thus the poet in Henry could feel, and try to equalize, unspeakable grief with spoken beauty.

Fortunately, the quiet of homely events followed the two tragic blows. Henry labored at the Emerson chores, wrote for *The Dial*, read his papers at the Lyceum, and participated in the gatherings of Emerson's talkative friends. But something had gone out of his life there. It is true, he felt closer to Lidian now, doubly tied by death as well as by life. She was deeply sympathetic, and possessed a useful sense of humor. This came out in a letter to her husband, in which she reported a Conversation he had missed. She stood up for Henry, who was "brave and noble, well as I have always liked him, he still grows on me."

Nature was now Henry's chief resource. Nature held firm, did not go back on him, and the part of nature that died was resurrected at the coming of spring. He confessed to being "still of Nature the child," and said, "If I were a physician I would try my patients thus. I would wheel them to the window and let Nature feel their pulse."

The woods offered Henry exercise for his fancy, as well as for his legs. When he saw a fox's trail stretching a quarter of a mile across the pond, he was curious to know what had determined its graceful curvatures. "Surely they were coincident with the fluctuations of some mind. . . . If these things are not to be called up and accounted for in the Lamb's Book of Life, I shall set them down for careless accountants. Here was one expression of the divine mind this morning. The pond was his journal, and last night's snow a *tabula rasa*"—a clean slate for him.

When Henry saw the fox sixty rods ahead, he gave chase. "I tossed my head aloft and bounded away, snuffing the air like a foxhound, and spurning the world and the Humane Society at each bound. It seemed the woods rang with the hunter's horn, and Diana and all the satyrs joined in the chase and cheered with me. Olympian and Elean youths were waving palms on the hills." (Henry couldn't quite leave the Harvard Library behind!)

The fox eluded Henry, who, "hoping this experience would prove a useful lesson to him, returned to the village by the highway of the river."

As the months passed at this pleasant job of being handyman to his famous friend, Henry felt with increasing certainty that he was marking time. He had been invited to stay a year and had already spent two years under that hospitable roof. His gains had been great. He was able to refer to Emerson (in a letter to Lidian later) as his "friend and brother." He had come to regard Emerson's wife with deep affection. He had seen his thoughts in print, though not for pay.

Yet to what end? In nature everything grew from stage to stage. How much more natural, then, for a human being blest with consciousness to do the same? What was the next stage for him? He asked himself this question with an increasing irritability that showed in his relations to the household, until even Emerson saw that an end had arrived. And, as had been the case so many times before, he was able to open a door for his protégé.

Emerson's brother William and his family lived on Staten Island, in New York Harbor. If Henry were engaged to tutor Haven, William's son, he would be able to visit editors in New York and perhaps gain a foothold as a writer. Waldo wrote William, who acceded to his brother's request. And so it came about that Henry, rather ruefully, packed his few belongings in preparation for venturing forth at last into the big world.

SEVEN

The New York Intermission

"THIS is no way to spend May Day," Henry said to his father as they were waiting for the stage.

"Any other young man of twenty-six who found himself shifted from a village to New York City would consider himself fortunate. You will have woods on Staten Island, and live near the ocean. For the price of a ferry ticket, you can visit the magazine editors. Have you forgotten your object in going?"

"No, I am to apprentice myself to selling myself," Henry replied out of an acquired clarity of insight.

"Ellery Channing approves, Son. He says you should not see Concord again for ten years and should grind up fifty Concords in your mill—whatever he may mean by that."

"He means that New York is fifty times the size of Concord and that I am to devour and digest it. I see it differently. Unless Concord, in my person, can conquer New York, I am lost."

John Thoreau changed the subject. "Mr. Emerson was good enough to say to your mother that his brother hopes Haven Emerson will absorb some of the Concord atmosphere."

"Then he should come where he could inhale it on the spot."

Fortunately, the stage drew up then, and Henry's father said, "Our love goes with you, Son. May success be yours."

Henry had made up his mind about true success. It was to advance confidently in the direction of one's dreams. Even to be on the right road, in this world of a thousand confusions, was success. A man had to succeed alone before he could enjoy his success with others. If New York City allowed him to do this on an expanded plane, well and good; but he had his doubts.

Henry's first days in the William Emerson household confirmed these forebodings. He disliked the novel atmosphere of wealth, with its set of values which he disdained. The New York accent fell on material success and grim competition with other material interests.

Then Haven Emerson, in Henry's outdoor eyes, was no boy at all, but a carefully dressed manikin. "I am not attracted to him," Henry wrote of his charge. "He shall frequent me, as much as he can, and I'll be I." This take-it-or-leave-it attitude would have won no boy, however dressed. And Haven soon discovered how dire a threat to his fun this upcountry fellow promised to be. Mr. Thoreau wanted to trot him off into the woods. Luckily for Haven, his tutor came down with bronchitis, brought on by the stuffiness of the house. This was followed by a lingering indisposition which did not improve Henry's temper. He turned sarcastic about Haven's civilized amusements and would have none of them.

May passed, and June, July, and August, and Henry's

homesickness remained as acute as ever. He writes it out as follows in this letter:

Staten Island, August 6, 1843.

Dear Mother,

I think of you all very often, and wonder if you are separated from me only by so many miles of earth, or so many miles of memory. This life we live is a strange dream, and I don't believe at all any account men give of it. Methinks I should be content to sit at the back door in Concord, under the poplar tree, henceforth forever. . . .

The letter goes on to picture with acute nostalgia a Sunday evening at home. His Staten Island experiment was proving to Henry Thoreau that his roots and being were inextricably fixed in Concord and that he could not be exported or transplanted. It also proved that he could never adjust to the life of the bustling mercantile metropolis across the Bay. On paydays, he took the ferry to Manhattan and proffered the letters of introduction that Waldo Emerson had supplied. He talked with Henry James, the father of Henry James the novelist, and the two got on well. Henry wrote home that this apostle of Swedenborg made "humanity seem more erected and respectable. I was never more kindly and faithfully catechized. He is a man, and takes his own way, or stands still in his own place. I know of no one so patient and determined to have the good of you." In other words, a sort of male Aunt Mary Emerson. "He wants an expression of your faith, or to be sure that it is a faith, and confesses that his own treads fast upon the neck of his understanding."

How clearly Henry outlines his own character when depicting another! That praise of Henry James was warmth indeed, and one might think that a city which bred and housed so worthy a man would be saved in Henry's eyes. Yet so oppressed did the Concord youth feel that he was soon writing in his Journal, "Who can see these cities and say that there is any life in them? I walked through New York yesterday—and met no real and living person."

That venom was drawn from one so obstinately blind that a hasty judgment of Henry Thoreau would dismiss him as stupid egotist. William Emerson was patient with him for Waldo's sake, but after one such supercilious remark, Mr. Emerson read him a long overdue lecture. "How can you draw the good from people, Henry, unless you open them up? From what my brother tells me, you take so true an interest in the trappers and ditchers in Concord that they reveal themselves to you. Of course you think our city mean if you pass by with downcast eyes and speak to none."

One rebuke was unlikely to throw Henry off center and he was soon waxing caustic again. He called one editor "a concave man, and you see by his attitude and the lines of his face that he is retreating from himself and from yourself with sad doubts."

To retreat from oneself was, in Henry's eyes, the unforgivable sin, because if the man would not be himself, who would be? The Concord rebel's error lay in the fact that he wished others to act in accordance with *his* wisdom, which would have amounted to a retreat from *themselves*. It is very difficult to make the world over in one's own image, especially if the would-be savior is a country jack aged twenty-six with a gift for sarcasm.

However, Henry did like Horace Greeley, editor of the New York *Tribune*. Greeley was a hearty New Hampshire-born man, whose motto was, "Now be neighborly," and who recognized at once the merit of the Thoreau prose, after Henry showed him a few of his *Dial* pieces. A useful connection between New Yorker and Concordian was established, and Greeley not only bought some of Henry's work but later became his ardent promoter.

Another newspaperman, Albert Brisbane, did not please Henry, who thought, "He looks like a man who has lived in a cellar, far gone in consumption."

One wonders what Waldo Emerson thought of his protégé, when he received such nonsense as this in a letter from Henry, "The city is a thousand times meaner than I could have imagined. The pigs in the street are the most respectable part of the population. When will the world learn that a million men are of no importance compared with one man?" And one might add, When will a young man cease damning a city's population because it does not measure up to his personal philosophy? Henry was too enraged to see that the pigs, which admittedly lived up to their nature, were in the end only wholeheartedly being pigs, while the despised New Yorkers were busily engaged in equally individual enterprises, some of which were educational, humanitarian, artistic, spiritual, and destined to make their country the envied destination of those desiring the freedom to be themselves—Henry's own mission. He was too angry, sick, and uncertain to realize that the blindest man of all is he who will not see.

William Emerson, the patient, tried once more to open

Henry's eyes, saying, "You are engaged in a boxing match against the city. Why not look for the good in us, and let the rest go? Force yourself to criticize justly, instead of in such sweeping statements.

"I was not born to be forced. I will breathe after my own fashion," declared the country individualist. "Let us see who is strongest."

It was no use. Henry was not born even to be persuaded. William Emerson induced him to go hear the Quaker reformer, Lucretia Mott. He was struck by the Quaker uniformity of style, the women "looking all like sisters or so many chickadees," and the men's square coats and expansive hats bearing their own testimony to lack of vain show.

Henry the reformer did not warm up to other reformers, however. In October, he wrote to his sister Helen, "My objection to Channing and all that fraternity is that they need and deserve sympathy themselves rather than are able to render it to others. They want faith, and mistake their private ail for an infected atmosphere. . . . I have the jaundice myself, but I also know what it is to be well."

So possibly this painful sojourn in New York was helping Henry to open his eyes wider. But he failed in his immediate objective—to place himself in the publishing world. He submitted pieces of his writing which were returned. He interviewed editors "and discussed their affairs with them. Some propose to me to do what an honest man cannot. Among others I conversed with the Harpers—to see if they might not find me useful to them but they say they are making $50,000 annually, and their motto is to let well alone. I find that I talk with these poor men as if I were over head and heels in business, and a few thousands were no consideration to me."

Humor is salvation, and while it could not make Henry a New Yorker, it kept him from despair. It was slowly borne in on him that he was an exile from all that he truly loved. His disheartenment gnawed at his physical vitals and that wholeness of his daily mood on his river. Where your heart is your treasure is, and he asked himself what he was doing, seeking his treasure in this heartless city?

He had relearned the lesson he had thought he knew: "Every man's success is in proportion to his *average* ability," he had told his Journal. In this stone prison he could not utilize his abilities. He would no longer try to live the life as ordered by others. He would return to Concord, strengthened in his determination—*to live his own life.*

EIGHT

A Fresh Start

WHILE Henry was ill, before going to Staten Island, he wrote in his Journal, "What am I at present? A diseased bundle of nerves standing between time and eternity like a withered leaf. A more miserable object one could not well imagine."

No wonder he was willing to try anything, even the city, which was the sum of all that he detested. On returning to his beloved Concord, he wrote, "We may waive just so much care of ourselves as we devote of care elsewhere." A true observation which might be called the Golden Rule of Happiness. In care-laden New York he had focused his attention on getting ahead, like the urban multitudes whom he considered unalive. When he re-entered the family and shared their cares again, he cast off much of his fretful self-concern.

His father had tired of paying rent for the imposing Parkman House and had bought a lot on the far side of the new railroad tracks. One day Henry met Sam Staples, who kept Concord's jail, and knew from the glint in this hearty country fellow's eye that he was in for a ribbing. These two had done some surveying together and liked each other. Staples was quick, clear, downright, well-meaning but fond of poking fun, and now he said, "I hear you're going to move again, Henry."

"It's Father's way of seeing the country," Henry said dryly. "But this time we're going to dig in."

A lounger asked, "Whar you movin' to, Texas?" The country beyond the tracks seemed equally remote. Other loafers heard and laughed and repeated the joke until the name stuck.

"Your pa must like the smell of cinders," Staples commented.

"He's tired of boarders," Henry said, and could have added that land was cheap in "Texas."

During the months after Henry's escape from New York, he helped with the pencil making that kept the family going, and got a taste of commercial rivalry. William Monroe, who had set up Mr. Thoreau in the business, was worrying about loss of his own markets and tried to stop Ebenezer Wood from supplying materials which the Thoreaus needed. Monroe failed, but the threat remained. Henry tried using other ingredients, while at the same time simplifying the machinery. He also invented a method of grinding the old material finer, thus giving a smoother substance. Had Henry been less Olympian and more materially ambitious, he could no doubt have become a successful businessman—like any New Yorker. As it was, he kept his ingredients and processes secret, and presently the Thoreau pencil making was yielding a moderately good income.

Henry varied his activities that winter of 1843-44. He was made curator of the Concord Lyceum, and the town gave him $109 for expenses. Of this, frugal Henry spent only $100 in providing the hall, heating and lighting, and twenty-five lecturers. Some distinguished men gave their services. Henry induced his New York friend, Horace Greeley, to journey to Concord and lecture. Also, he procured such stars as George Bancroft, Theodore Parker, Wendell Phillips, James Freeman Clarke, and Emerson.

In New York, Henry had eased his homesickness by writing outdoor papers, and *The Dial* printed "A Winter Walk" after Emerson had done considerable blue-penciling on the manuscript. Editor Emerson wrote to the author, "I had some hesitation about accepting it, notwithstanding its faithful observation, and its fine sketches of the pickerel fisher and the wood-chopper, on account of *mannerism,* an old charge of mine—as if, by attention, one could get the trick of rhetoric; as, for example, to call a cold place sultry, a solitude public, a wilderness *domestic* (a favorite word), and in the the woods to insult over cities, armies, etc. By pretty free omissions, however, I have removed my principal objections."

What Henry thought of having his style tamed so is not known, but can be guessed, since no true writer enjoys amputations or face-changings without the anesthesia of his consent.

With spring, Henry was heaving manure, digging the cellar for the Texas house, and frequenting his river haunts. In April, during a hot dry spell, he and Edward Hoar, a Harvard student at that time, decided to row up the Sudbury River for a day's escape from Concord's mild civilization. This was a censurable act on Henry's part, in the opinion of the citizens, for that was the day set for Town Meeting, the annual business meeting at which anyone with a civic conscience must be present and discuss the past and future expenditures of tax money. Henry's "signing-off" of church was bad enough, while to abdicate his responsibility for bettering the life of Concord seemed untrustworthiness itself. But the most irate Concordian could hardly have wished on Henry the mental suffering that he was to endure on that day. It is still recollected in the town a century and a quarter later.

Henry has laid bare what happened and what he felt about it in a long and vivid Journal entry. He and Edward took fishing tackle "that we might fitly procure our food from the stream, Indian-like." But Henry forgot to take matches— a strange omission for a camper—and borrowed one from a shoemaker.

Fish were caught, and, in spite of the exceeding dryness of woods and grass, a fire was kindled on a stump, of all places! Dry grass grew about the stump, from which sparks were readily blown, and so was kindled the fire that was to burn over a hundred acres of woodland and even threaten Concord village itself.

Henry's factual account of the growing conflagration, of the residents' feelings, and of his own incredible reactions to the havoc is at once a striking piece of reporting and an unveiling of the tortured being who had set his beloved woods afire. He tries to hide his anguish in bravado. "I said to myself, 'who are these men who are said to be owners of these woods, and how am I related to them? I have set fire to the forest, but I have done no wrong therin, and now it is as if the lightning had done it. These flames are but consuming their natural food.' "

Spent with running, he climbed to the highest rock of Fair Haven Cliff. After he heard the distant bell of Concord giving the fire alarm, he watched the destructive flames approach and ate his heart in bitterness. When about to be surrounded by the fire, he joined the workers, who finally saved Concord by setting backfires and digging trenches.

Henry noticed that "the crowd who were so ready to condemn the individual who had kindled the fire did not sympathize with the owners of the woods, but in fact were highly elate and, as it were, thankful for the opportunity which had afforded them so much sport; and it was only half a dozen owners, so called, though not all of them, who looked sour or grieved, and I felt that I had a deeper interest in the woods, knew them better and should feel their loss more, than any or all of them."

That night, he watched the dying fire past midnight, and finally threaded his way "to the spot where the fire had taken, and discovered the now broiled fish,—which had been dressed —scattered over the burnt grass."

Henry did not entrust this fateful day to his Journal until six years after the fire. The subject was too close to his heart, for all of his pretended unconcern. The neighbors would not let him forget that he had burnt up their property; he himself could not forget the loss of his treasure, the wild.

That same dire month of April, Emerson decided to let *The Dial* die, for want of support. The public did not know of it, and the few subscribers did not become the many. So Henry was bereft of a mouthpiece. His thoughts, gathered from fields and woods and river, had become lectures, then essays, and some of them had found the slightly larger public of

The Dial. Well, he could still try writing a book. The New
York foray had not only scattered his energies but his mind,
his very aim. Fortunately, he needed only to read his Journal
to find himself again—the essence of himself at his best.
Now, turning the pages over, he read, "Follow your genius
closely enough, and it will not fail to show you a fresh prospect every hour."

That was it! The Texas house was about finished. He
would hive-up somewhere and write a book out of his convictions, have something to show for himself, get away from
his townsmen's taunts and the family's wish that he might
marry.

He had heard Sam Staples talking to his father outside
the pencil shop, and he was in it. Sam said, "I was hoping
Henry'd bring back a bride from New York. She'd take his
mind off all this talk about the fire."

"There might as well have been no women in New York,
for all the impression they made on Henry," Mr. Thoreau
replied dryly.

"Someone should call his attention to them," Sam said.

"It would do no good. Henry is not inclined that way. He
looks to them for intellect."

Sam knew that this was affectionate joking on Mr.
Thoreau's part. In that household, Henry could do no wrong.

"Well, you don't have to worry about him, like some
fathers."

"I do worry, Sam. Henry is twenty-seven and talks about
enjoying life to its core—as if a good half of life wasn't
woman and marriage. Why, women know life as birds know
the air."

"It's these bookish men Henry keeps company with, sir. To listen to Mr. Alcott or to Mr. Emerson, you'd be led to believe that life's a peg to hang ideas on. When I see Mr. Emerson going by, it's like the sun coming out of a cloud. But I don't envy him. No, sir. He knows all about the Almighty but doesn't give thanks for a pretty girl's smile, and Henry takes after him."

"Not one of my children shows the slightest inclination to marriage, Sam. Helen and Sophia seem content with spinsterhood, and now Henry is talking of buying a wood lot somewhere to share with the owls. My wife and I would like the sight of a grandchild before we die."

"Well, Mr. Thoreau, I never saw a home where each was so fond of the others. Henry's eyes will open yet. Lots of young men don't marry until they're thirty."

"I do not complain. It's only that I wish Henry not to miss the happiness I've had in my home, though so little earned. Henry is a dutiful son, sober and industrious and with a head on him we do not yet fully appreciate. The house is like a stove without coals in it when he's gone."

At this point the talkers moved away and Henry stiffened; he had heard it all before. How little even those who lived almost in one's pocket did know! Was he so hard to read aright? Had he not offered marriage to Ellen Sewall in the hope of such a home with her? Was not the feeling of life he had for Lucy Brown the supreme emotion which the poets called love? And what of Lidian Emerson? The thought of her constantly elevated his life. His heart answered to her heart. A gentle spirit, a wise spirit, a loving spirit. He went to his room at the thought of her and read again the letter he had never sent: "When I love you I feel as if I were annexing another world to mine. Whom I know as an atmosphere. Whom in thought my spirit continually embraces. Unto whom I flow. Who art all that I can imagine—my inspirer. The feminine of me. On the remembrances of whom I repose."

They do not know me, Henry thought. It is my fault. If only they could know me, they might still blame me on many another count, but not for being cold of heart.

His ferment of meditation was interrupted by Ellery Channing, who was full of a proposed walking trip through the Catskill Mountains, and would Henry go with him?

Henry agreed, to Channing's surprise, and they took the trip. But it was merely a stopgap, not a solution to Henry's restlessness. At heart, he was deeply the yea-sayer to life, despite his savage comments on people's abuse of living. He knew that a sure remedy for his present thwarted feeling was to name one's obstacles, drag them out into the open, and then try to surmount them. He wrote this self-advice down to remind himself of the never-failing cure, "Be resolutely and faithfully what you are, and the rest will come right."

But what *was* he? A lover of living and a journalist of his loves. But precisely what did he love? Health and integrity and nature and nature's God and good writing and the wisdom hid in libraries. He loved a few people almost wholly, others in part, and he felt pity for the rest, and an indignation because they cheated themselves of life. What did he hate? Commercialism, and the near-sightedness of most people about life, and the meanness he felt for himself when he fell back from his highest thought. And particularly this indecision.

136

A FRESH START

As the winter of 1844-45 passed, Henry's resolve deepened: no longer would he put off writing his book, so long dormant in his mind and made imperative by John's death. On the surface, it would seem to be a log of the river trip with John. Below the surface, it would collect his truest thoughts about friendship and love and other matters too long unexpressed. He must have unlimited leisure, while earning the minimum of cash for barest necessities, and unbothered by the incessant talk of his affectionate family. The Irish laborers who had worked on the railroad had left their makeshift huts here and there; he might live in one of them for next to nothing.

Henry remembered visiting Stearns Wheeler, his classmate at Harvard, who had built a shack on Flint Pond, in Lincoln township nearby. Channing had suggested the same sort of retreat. After word had reached him that Henry was meditating a move to the woods, Channing wrote from New York, "I see nothing for you on this earth but that field I once christened 'Briars'; go out upon that, build yourself a hut, and there begin the grand process of devouring yourself alive. Eat yourself up; you will eat nobody else, nor anything else."

As so often happens to a hunted man, an unforeseen way of escape opens in the line of his deepest nature—opens naturally, with so forceful a logic that the required step to safety, which looked so improbable, becomes clear, inevitable. And so was it with Henry in his dark hour.

Nothing could have been more natural than for Emerson to want to own a place on Walden Pond, not much over a mile away from his home. There he could always find the silence, solitude, and the caressing beauty which invited pondering over his next essay. Having chanced to run into the owner of a part of Walden's shore who wanted to sell, Emerson bought eleven acres at $8.10 an acre. It was rich in briar patches, and a harvest of blackberries would delight Henry, who still liked to take children berrying.

The day after the sale, Emerson heard that Heartwell Bigelow, who owned the land adjoining his newly bought property, might convert all those beautiful pines into lumber. Henry was present and urged Emerson to lay out the $125 asked for this three-acre wood lot. Henry by now had decided that Walden Pond would furnish a suitable location for his hideout, and, while Emerson did not approve of his young friend cutting himself off from society, he did save the pines by purchasing them, and then offered his new domain to Henry as a hut site, on condition that he clear the field of undergrowth. Emerson's other condition was that, if his tenant vacated these wild premises, he must sell any improvements to him. Henry, who believed in being debtor to none, gladly assented.

So, by March of 1845, the way was at last clear for Henry to try his new experiment in living.

NINE

Trial by Self-Reliance

WALDEN POND one might call a gift of Providence, so essential was it to Henry Thoreau in his life crisis and so important to American literature has it been ever since.

Like most providential offerings, it had lain close at hand all the while, a mile and a half from the center of Concord, and less distant than that from the Thoreaus' Texas house, by way of the Fitchburg railroad tracks.

Henry vented a good deal of sarcasm on the railroad, which reached Concord in 1844. "We do not ride on the railroad, it rides on us," he complained. But, as so often is the case with scoffers who make sweeping accusations, he benefited by that which he had denounced. The trains' right of way afforded him a short cut for his hundreds of visits home. The Deep Cut near his hut fed his imagination—and Journal. And if the railroad had not come, the Irish immigrants would not have been needed as laborers, and he could not have housed himself in one of their abandoned shanties so cheaply.

Strangely, he borrowed the ax with which he began clearing the Emerson property from the one man who seems to us unlikely—Bronson Alcott—and set to work with as whole a heart as he had had in years. When Emerson strolled out to see how his friend was getting on, he was struck anew by the character evident in all the young man was and did.

Henry, now nearly twenty-eight, was in his physical prime. His body looked well-knit, strong and lithe. His chin, as Emerson remarked, was firm enough to hammer honor home like a nail. His mouth kept no Puritan line, having a full lower lip and a Cupid's bow. Passion was there, Emerson thought, but no tepid hair-trigger emotion. How had the young man carved out so much determination as his face and figure expressed? Even he, Waldo Emerson, saw no such ruggedness of will when he gazed in his shaving glass. Yet Henry's mien was not dour. He laughed often, a fact frequently forgotten, even by his admirers. He laughed long, sometimes boisterously, oftener quietly, and now and then in scorn—also slyly, when the humor in him had not reached words.

He had chosen the site for his shelter in March, as soon as the snow vacated it—a gently falling, south-facing slope—and he had felled a few tall arrow-straight young pines for timber. He dug his cellar where a woodchurck had formerly hollowed out its burrow, six feet square and seven feet deep, below the frost line—in two hours.

Thoreau is pronounced *thorough* in his native region and Henry lived his name, that is, thoroughly. He followed out a thought to its end and made a universal of it, and his mind was not happy until it had stored the final form of his thought in that cellar called his Journal, where it would be preserved against mankind's forgetfulness.

As he sweated with his shovel, it pleased him to realize that the most splendid of city houses had cellars under them, and after this structure had disappeared, the dent in the earth would still be seen. "The house is still but a sort of porch at the entrance of a burrow."

Emerson announced that a scholar must not dig, but must save the cream of his strength for his work, that it might show the utmost vigor. Henry got his thoughts while working—or walking—and worked them up in his Journal later. His style was more muscular and vigorous than Emerson's. His page is filled with sights, sounds, smells, and his ideas are stained with sweat. Henry dug up his facts while excavating a cellar, or cut them down as he felled the pines, and made his prose of them. Both men had the idealist's imagination, but each housed it differently in words. They were as different, humanly and intellectually, as the two sides of a silver dollar—and as related. They were lifelong friends at heart, yet neither wholly satisfied the other.

One day before the ice left Walden Pond, Henry regretted borrowing that ax from Alcott—who had made a fuss over the loan. He admitted that it was unwise to begin by borrowing, but he was adept at making philosophical excuses for his acts, and noted that borrowing was the most generous course to pursue, since it permitted one's fellow men to take an interest in one's enterprise!

The reason for his regret was a major mishap—the axhead flew off. Henry cut a green hickory for a wedge, drove it into the halve with a stone, let it soak in a pond hole so that the wood might swell, and noticed a striped snake sliding into the water. It lay on the bottom, "apparently without inconvenience," for a quarter of an hour, and suggested to the watchful philosopher that men might continue in their semi-torpid condition, "but if they should feel the influence of the spring of springs arousing them, they would of necessity rise to a higher and more ethereal life." So, thanks to Alcott's characteristically imperfect ax, Henry had a fresh view of the resurrection.

Possibly it advised Henry that great writing followed the same course: lying half asleep in the mind until "the influence of the spring of springs" suddenly lifts it into literature. The book *Walden* was to become such fruit.

When Henry needed boards, he visited James Collins, an Irishman who had worked on the railroad and lived in a shanty, "considered an uncommonly fine one." Henry's page about this purchase—possibly the only dwelling a needy writer has procured for $4.25—shows the humorous fellow he was at heart. His humor was not invented, nor even a distortion of the facts. It is a straight-faced bringing-out of the comical aspect of the facts, as when Henry describes his bargain with Collins, "he to vacate at five tomorrow morning, selling to nobody else meanwhile, I to take possession at six. It were well, he said, to be there early, and anticipate certain indistinct but wholly unjust claims on the score of ground rent and fuel. This, he assured me, was the only encumberance. At six, I passed him and his family on the road. One large bundle held their all,—bed, coffee-mill, looking-glass, hens—all but the cat; she took to the woods and became a wild cat, and, as I learned afterward, trod in a trap set for woodchucks, and so became a dead cat at last." Henry proved a thousand times over that real humor and the human condition go hand in hand.

He drew the shanty's nails, carted the boards home, as he

now thought of his site, and, with some friends helping, as May began, set up the frame of the house. It was made weatherproof, with the boards feather-edged and lapped. Henry laid the chimney foundation by lugging two cartloads of stones from the water edge up the slope in his arms—and moved in.

Only experienced campers can realize Henry Thoreau's contentment on that midsummer night, after his guests had left, as he went to bed in the benign quiet of his self-made home. No boarders would interrupt his thoughts at breakfast. He would have only his own few chores to do. A quarter hour would suffice to make his bed, wash his plate and spoon, carry in wood, and sweep the floor.

He had still the plastering to do to make his refuge storm-proof. He had planted two and one-half acres of the briar-patch clearing with beans, corn, turnips, and potatoes. They would have to be hoed and the pine stumps pried from the ground to light a year of fires. But most of the day would be his to explore the region, watch his four-footed neighbors—and think.

Thoughts were to be his chief crop, and the only frost that crop need fear was the chill of boarding-house prattle. Aunt Louisa, complaining of her lumbago, could wilt a whole sowing of reflections. The incessant suggestions that he do this or that were more destructive to mental fruitage than six woodchucks among the beans. Like dreams, new thoughts could vanish from one's memory unless *entertained*. Then they brought others with them, making the day's value. Great thoughts hallowed the day they came, although one spent it heaving manure.

Indeed, one's thoughts are the measure of one's world, and part of the meaning of the world. It was necessary to use some part of the world as a symbol to express his thoughts, and experience led the way to that end. A man was as rich as his thoughts, or as poor, and Henry intended to be very rich. That would be a joke on his neighbors, who at that very moment were saying, "Poor Henry, living in his shanty little better than a woodchuck!"

Henry had heard them say just that before he had lived at Walden Pond for a week. One day he saw a woodchuck crossing a field and decided to interview the animal, to find out precisely what his opinions were. The report of the questioner's findings makes one of the most illuminating entries in the Journal. Henry talked "to him *quasi* forest lingo, baby-talk, at any rate in a conciliatory tone," and convinced the woodchuck of his good intentions. The emanations from Henry's sincere love of the wild and its creatures had a mesmeric influence on the chuck, who permitted the man to fondle it as he noted every aspect of the creature.

Many of Henry's neighbors found him cold, a sort of glacial boulder planted in the human pasture. The few who knew him well called it his reserve. Why did he reserve part of himself? Because he had found out that part of him was unwanted, was laughable, foolish, dangerous, and irritating to most human beings. But toward nature and her innocents, the animals, Henry had no reserves. He loved nature as most people love themselves, with a wholehearted attachment. The part of nature that could return his feeling, often did so, although hesitantly, from long experience with these two-footed monsters who were forever hunting them down, but with a trustfulness that Henry never outraged.

He had the same warmth of feeling for children, nature's creatures not yet trained into worldliness by their elders. And so children loved him. Emerson's equation, "Love and you shall be loved," worked like a natural law when permitted.

The need was to be simple, whole, natural, honest as a ray of light, and Heaven knew how wide the expanse one ray could illumine. So Henry began his fresh start at Walden Pond, a retraining in simplicity, with such a light heart and joy that it re-created him. The illnesses of Staten Island were forgotten, and his twenty-six months at Walden were radiant with health.

His days were active but they were not crowded, and it was on their broad margin that he wrote one of American literature's happiest books, *A Week on the Concord and Merrimack Rivers*. He wrote it as a memorial to the love of his brother and in it he expressed his long-held convictions about friendship. His feeling bore him to altitudes that appear snow-clad and solitary; but then Henry meant these pages to last. He *believed* in friendship as his neighbors believed in saving their lives—and he lived up to his belief. Since his friends did not, perhaps could not, live according to his belief, and even though they lived sincerely according to their own, his friendships failed him in the higher reaches of his demands. Yet it is possible that they gave him much happiness on less than the ultimate levels. And he had the immense satisfaction of putting the blueprint of idealized friendship on paper.

The new householder furnished his abode with three

chairs—"one for myself, two for company, three for society."
He sat often on the grass, for people fairly thronged to him,
from the idly curious to his literary companions. In this
Walden chapter on "Visitors" he says, "I think that I love
society as much as most, and am ready enough to fasten
myself like a bloodsucker for the time to any full-blooded
man that comes my way. I am naturally no hermit."

Yet it has been difficult to shatter the image of Henry
the Hermit. Legends wear away in time, but facts must
struggle long and hard to demolish them. The facts have been
available for a hundred years: Henry liked to be alone part
of every day; he craved immersion in nature part of every
day; he considered people unwise if they kept their noses to
the business grindstone overlong; he abominated other kinds
of slavery; his ambition was to write; he trained himself to see
with penetration and describe vividly; he phrased his ripened
thoughts with such individual precision that they are collected
by connoisseurs as he collected arrowheads; he maintained his
identity against all pressures with the integrity of the oak trees
he loved; and, finally, he has been found worthy of the
American Hall of Fame—a reward delayed for two or three
lifetimes because of the legend.

The proofs of his love of society are sometimes surprising,
even to those who think they know Henry's life well. It is
hard *not* to think of his life at Walden Pond as solitary. Yet
his withdrawal from Concord was the talk of the village, and
the curious walked or drove out to Walden to see what the
young man was up to now. His friends walked that easy
mile for a chat. Prudence Ward wrote in a letter dated January 20, 1846, "He has many visitors, whom he receives with

pleasure & does his best to entertain. We talk of passing the day with him." And this in New England's January! What then of June?

June supplied hordes. Henry wrote, "It is surprising how many great men and women a small house will contain. I have had twenty-five or thirty souls, with their bodies, at once under my roof." He adds, typically, "And yet we often parted without being aware that we had come very near to one another."

His "best" room, his withdrawing room, was the pine wood outside the house.

> Thither in summer days, when distinguished guests came, I took them, and a priceless domestic swept the floor and dusted the furniture and kept the things in order.
>
> If one guest came he sometimes partook of my frugal meal, and it was no interruption to conversation to be stirring a pasty-pudding, or watching the rising and maturing of a loaf of bread in the ashes, in the meanwhile. But if twenty came and sat in my house there was nothing said about dinner, though there might be bread enough for two, more than if eating were a forsaken habit; but we naturally practiced abstinence, and this was never felt to be an offense against hospitality, but the most proper and considerate course.

Henry was often a guest in Concord homes. At last the village was interested in its son. In *Walden* he wrote, "Some have asked what I got to eat; if I did not feel lonesome, if I was not afraid, and the like. Others have been curious to learn what portion of my income I devoted to charitable purposes; and some, who have large families, how many poor people I maintained." There is his humor at its quietest, and funniest.

He made one fatal mistake in his chapter "Economy." He set down his expenses to the last ¾ of a cent, but omitted mention of the free meals in Concord and the pies his mother gave him. The omission of those pies has condemned Henry forever in the eyes of housekeepers. They refuse to read the writings of anyone so utterly dishonest. They warm with instant indignation at mention of his name. Then they remember his other dereliction, his bachelorhood, and slam the door in his face. Gradually, it is fair to add, a matching ability to parry and thrust with wit has developed in the long struggle against condemnation, and a younger, broader-minded generation of the feminine sex is enjoying his sarcasm and quoting his sharp-edged good sense.

Great books are not written on the spot, for truth requires testing and takes a period to sink in. Time is needed to supply the writer wih perspective, and only reflection can ratify an experience.

Two years before going to Walden, Henry said to Emerson, "In writing, conversation should be folded many times thick. It is the height of art that, on the first perusal, plain common sense should appear; on the second, severe truth; and on a third, beauty; and, having these warrants for its depth and reality, we may then enjoy the beauty for evermore."

If it takes three readings to discover the whole of a great

piece of writing, it requires at least as many writings, unless the composition has been accomplished in the writer's mind before being set down. Henry Thoreau is so memorable because he wrote and rewrote and further worked over a sentence until it became wholly his own, and therefore new. The book *Walden* is one long broad vein of gold-bearing ore, rich in nuggets of wit and proven good sense on every page:

"Every man is the builder of a temple, called his body."

"That man is richest whose pleasures are the cheapest."

"Our life is frittered away by detail . . . simplify, simplify."

"To be awake is to be alive."

"Goodness is the only investment that never fails."

It was not *Walden* but *A Week on the Concord and Merrimack Rivers* that Henry was piecing together from his Journal and memories at the Pond. He had no lock on the door, but he did keep his Journal and manuscript in a locked box. His brother John must have lived again with him during the snowy nights of recalling that September voyage.

Of necessity, the rivalry for Ellen Sewall was remembered: "I dreamed this night of an event which had occurred long before. It was a difference with a Friend, which had not ceased to give me pain, though I had no cause to blame myself. But in my dream ideal justice was at length done me for his suspicions, and I received that compensation which I had never obtained in my waking hours. I was unspeakably soothed and rejoiced, even after I awoke, because in dreams we never deceive ourselves, nor are deceived, and this seemed to have the authority of a final judgment."

Henry's reverie of friendship in the *Week* abruptly confronts the reader of the voyage as the first sight of Gibraltar must startle the Atlantic traveler. Henry capitalizes Friendship and Friend, as the old poets did Beauty and Truth. He speaks from his inmost heart, so passionately that embarrassed critics shrug off his delineation of this purest of loves as too far from daily reality to consider.

But then so is Shakespeare's delineation of Romeo's feelings. Henry's marvelous poem is not to be measured by the yardstick of prosaic habit. For every young man who has felt deeply toward another, Henry's account contains truths and revelations that point out the way to harmony in this relationship. It is a poet's handbook for ideal experience and gives inspired glimpses of "the fabulous retreating shores of some continent," which Henry calls "man."

"Friendship is evanescent in everyman's experience, and remembered like heat lightning in past summers."

"There is on earth no institution which Friendship has established; it is not taught by any religion; no scripture contains its maxims. It has no temple, nor even a solitary column."

"Of what use the friendliest disposition, even, if there are no hours given to Friendship, if it is forever postponed to unimportant duties and relations?"

"A Friend is one who incessantly pays us the compliment of expecting from us all the virtues, and who can appreciate them in us."

"My Friend is that one whom I can associate with my choicest thought."

"Friendship is not so kind as it is imagined; it has not much human blood in it."

"The only danger in Friendship is that it will end."

"But all that can be said of Friendship, is like botany to flowers."

These truths were wrung from Henry by hard experience. Sitting in his shelter on the nights of storm which protected him from his friends, for even that relationship can be overdone, Henry must have smiled at recalling how many of his neighbors thought him cold. He did not wear his heart on his sleeve. His loves, in the main, were not the sort that figured in romance. He loved his family throughout his life, helped it when needed, and was loved in return, which is a good sign of the genuineness of a love. He loved Concord's gifts to him and many of its people. He loved every aspect of nature in a degree hardly matched by any of his time. He loved the divinity encompassing the world and the universe, and was incapable of any profanation, as Emerson noted, by act or thought. And finally he confessed to his utter love of his life.

It was this intense passion for life and his willingness to sacrifice any obstacles to his enjoyment of it that made him wonder whether so many other people really did love being alive. If they did, how could they postpone living and bury their sense of life under such needless burdens? They needed more intelligent thinking or more courage to simplify themselves free. They took the roundabout way because it was customary. Henry said of the farmer, "To get his shoestrings he speculates in herds of cattle." Today, Henry Thoreau is called unrealistic, impractical, childish, blind, and, above all, selfish. He probably had no illusions as to his ability to reverse the course of society. But he had to utter the truth that was in him. If he could revive one other person's interest in independence, then *Walden* would be worthwhile writing.

A reform does not have to be total to have value, and Henry's account of life's renewal has stimulated readers ever since *Walden* appeared in print in 1854, seven years after he left Walden Pond. His chief article of faith was written to his friend, Harrison G. O. Blake, "What can be expressed in words can be expressed in life. . . . Did you ever hear of a man who had striven all his life faithfully and singly toward an object and in no measure obtained it? If a man constantly aspires, is he not elevated?"

In *Walden,* Henry was writing a parable, as indeed all writings that prove to be great and live are parables. They are fictions from which moral or spiritual truths are drawn. *Walden* had the advantage of being factual, more easily graspable, and could not be written off as a fairy tale. Its facts were true, for one, but the truths to be extracted were universal. The last thing Henry desired was to have imitators. What he did want was that each reader might find in its pages a new incentive to question his own conduct and decide whether he was actually realizing his true self. *Walden* was a guide to self-discovery.

Henry himself was still searching for the same imperative thing. "I long ago lost a hound, a bay horse, and a turtle-dove, and am still on their trail. Many are the travelers I have spoken to concerning them, describing their tracks and what calls they answered to. I have met one or two who had heard the hound, and the tramp of the horse, and even seen the dove disappear behind the cloud, and they seemed as anxious to recover them as if they had lost them themselves."

The proof that Henry was speaking to the human condition is found in *Walden's* longevity. It has never gone out of print.

The local inhabitants of Walden soon found Henry unobtrusive and began to be sociable. A wild native mouse, not found in the village, and ordinarily rather exclusive, built a nest under the house and adopted Henry. It ran up his clothes, even ran up the sides of the room, squirrel-like, by short spurts. Henry held cheese in his hand and this Daniel Boone of mice nibbled it, "and afterward cleaned his face and paws, like a fly, and walked away."

A phoebe built in Henry's woodshed, a robin in the pine beside the house, a partridge led her brood past the window, "clucking and calling to them like a hen, and in all her behavior proving herself the hen of the woods."

Henry marveled at the otter's ability to avoid being seen. "He grows to be four feet long, as big as a small boy, perhaps without any human being getting a glimpse of him." A raccoon frequented the woods behind the house. A woodcock and turtledoves visited the spring Henry dug nearby. He suspected, from the tracks discovered, that many a village hound "fit only to course a mud-turtle in a victualing cellar, sported his heavy quarters in the woods, without the knowledge of his master, and ineffectually sniffed at old fox burrows and woodchucks' hole, led perchance by some slight cur which nimbly threaded the woods."

Once Henry came upon a cat walking along the pond's stony shore. "The surprise was mutual. Nevertheless, the most domestic cat, which has lain on a rug all her days, appears quite at home in the woods, and by her sly and stealthy behavior, proves herself more native there than the regular inhabitants." One farmer's wife told him of a "winged cat" and described it so circumstantially that he supposed it to be part cat, part flying squirrel, and added, "This would have been the right kind of cat for me to keep, if I had kept any; for why should not a poet's cat be winged as well as his horse?"

In the fall, the loon came to molt and bathe in the pond, "making the woods ring with his wild laughter before I had risen." Henry tells of a game of loon-tag he played with one of these birds on a calm October noon. The visitor would laugh and dive and Henry try to guess where he would reappear and row there. He often guessed wrong and helped to widen the distance between them, whereupon the loon would appear and laugh "long and loud, and with more reason than before."

Henry was amazed how quickly the bird decided in which direction to go and put his resolve into execution. He would pass under Henry's boat, then stick his head out of the water to reconnoiter and instantly dive again. "But why, after displaying such cunning, did he invariably betray himself the moment he came up by that loud laugh? He was indeed a silly loon."

One day Henry witnessed a battle between two races of ants, red and black, and reported its progress with scientific care. "It was the only battle which I have ever witnessed, and the only battlefield I ever trod while the battle was raging." It reminded him of classic encounters, and he elevates it, with mock seriousness, to national levels. "For numbers and

carnage it was an Austerlitz or Dresden. Concord Fight! Two
killed on the patriots' side, and Luther Blanchard wounded!
Why, here every ant was a Buttrick,—'Fire! for God's sake
fire!'—and thousands shared the fate of Davis and Hosmer."

Henry noted a chip on which three ants were fighting,
carried it into the house and placed it under a tumbler on
his window sill, in order to see the issue. After an hour of
fierce combat, the black ant slowly chewed his foes to pieces.
Henry winds up the mock account by writing, "The battle
which I witnessed took place in the Presidency of Polk, five
years before the passage of Webster's Fugitive Slave Bill."

In these three battle-torn pages of *Walden* one glimpses
Henry's mind in action, as vigorous as the battlers' minds.
Here is the naturalist watching and describing with realistic
accuracy, the humorist magnifying the insect conflict to the
proportions of the American Revolution, with intent to
satirize the murderous folly of war. He first raises the "embattled insects to the importance of men in order to reduce
men to the level of insects," as Raymond Adams points out.
To complete the irony, Henry adds that historical reference
to the Fugitive Slave Bill, begot of Webster, the infamous
ruling that demanded the return of escaped slaves by any
and all in the North, however much they detested slavery.
Here we see a new Henry emerging.

It was Webster's hideous law which turned pacifist Henry
into a fighter against injustice. Justice was having a hard
time of it in the 1840's. The United States annexed Texas
in 1845, the year that Henry was practicing freedom by

erecting his hut. The Mexican War, which was in part used to extend slave-holding areas into the Southwest, was declared in May, 1846, and on Henry's visits to Concord, and in his home, he heard the antislavery cause more violently discussed than ever.

Late in July, 1846, when Henry was starting his second year at Walden, he walked in to Concord to pick up a shoe at the cobbler's—and was arrested by Sam Staples, his friend and fellow surveyor, for refusing to pay his poll tax.

The evening was warm, and so was the conversation. "When a sixth of the population of a nation which has undertaken to be the refuge of liberty are slaves, I think it is not too soon for honest men to rebel and revolutionize," was Henry's theme. By refusing to furnish one more dollar to buy a musket to shoot men with, Henry declared war on the United States Government. It was another ant-size war, if only size be considered, but with consequences that none could calculate.

The bystanders were on Staples' side. Here was this setter of forest fires, this loafer, living out there on that pond, as unsociable as a bear, and now refusing his dollar! Serve him right to be shut up.

Jailer Sam had no other course and Henry set down some earnest sarcasm later, calling the state half-witted and "timid as a lone woman with her silver spoons, and that it did not know its friends from its foes, and I lost all my remaining respect for it, and pitied it."

Henry's account of his night in jail is illuminating, both of himself and his experience, and when someone—probably an aunt—paid the tax dollar and fifty cents for fee,

Henry irately called it an "interference" and, "was mad as the devil," in Staples' words.

Emerson, as reported by Bronson Alcott, called Henry's act "mean and skulking and in bad taste," but he must have been impressed by the consequences of the jailing. For Henry wrote a hot-tempered lecture, entitled "The Rights and Duties of the Individual in Relation to Government," to make it clear that he had no desire not to serve the state in matters on which his conscience was clear. But he intended to keep his eye on the moral law and strive for absolute justice, truth, and the right. The source of these absolutes was, of course, God, Who operated through his, Thoreau's, conscience, in the latter's opinion. He did not begrudge the dollar, but it must be used for human betterment, not slavery. He had heard the American Revolution praised because of its faith in a man's unalienable right to life, liberty, and the pursuit of happiness. So it was unlikely that it was right to support a mistaken government in its effort to extinguish life, promote slavery instead of liberty, and end the happiness of millions.

When Henry published this lecture under the title "Civil Disobedience," he was speaking for *one,* the only one each man has it in him to assert, "It is not so important that many should be as good as you, as that there be some absolute goodness somewhere; for that will leaven the whole lump." "I was not born to be forced. I will breathe after my own fashion. . . . If a plant cannot live according to its nature, it dies; and so a man."

The Walden camper, in his most transcendental moments, could not have foreseen how it came to pass that his example, and the truth that issued from it, would "leaven the whole lump." His lonely resistance to the massed power of the state was, in the course of decades, to be heard round the world, as Emerson had said of the minutemen's shot. Gandhi made its principle the motive power for his campaign in India for Civil Resistance, whereby the meek came to inherit more of the earth than they could at once manage. One might say that Henry's night in jail had overthrown the British Empire, although the Muse of History might term that an over simplification.

Nor was Henry thinking in terms of empire. He was determined to keep his spiritual integrity, however overwhelming the powers aligned against him might appear—a Massachusetts David against a national Goliath. He wanted to pick blueberries with a clear conscience. He could not enjoy nature while some unworthy act vexed his spirit.

His feelings did experience a quick rebound after his return from the fetid jail to the sunlit waters of the waiting Pond. A plunge into its limpid clarity and coolness cleansed more than his body. He gave thanks for its refreshment and thought, "We are slow to realize water—the beauty and magic of it. It is interestingly strange to us forever. Immortal water, alive, sparkling with life, whereon was no trace of footstep."

He celebrated his liberation by taking the Emerson and Alcott youngsters berrying. Henry, who could be so dangerous to the state, was a born comrade for the child who entrusted its happiness to him. He knew an old road, where every bush and bramble was berry-heavy, and, like a flight of small birds, the children settled upon the riches, intent on sacking nature, Henry thought, like brigands or pillagers after a war.

When young Sam Hosmer stumbled and spilled his pail of berries, his distress was extreme, to the point of tears. The others ran to him and offered him berries so that he need not start picking again with an empty pail. But the disaster was too great for Sam to be consoled. So Henry put his arm about the troubled child and said, "If there are to be berries next year, Sam, some must be scattered. Nature has provided that a little boy should stumble, now and then, and sow berries on the soil. Now we shall have a grand crop of berries, Sammy, and we shall owe them to you."

Sam brightened, "Can I come and pick them?"

"For sure, and I shall bring you."

No wonder, after Henry's harrowing confrontation of the state, that he decided to seek wildness in its own haunts. On visits to his relatives in Bangor, Maine, he had sniffed the wild. Now he intended to immerse himself in the deep woods and climb Mount Katahdin, Maine's highest summit. He left Concord on the anniversary of the start of his river trip with John, and doubtless John traveled with him in spirit, for Henry's great loves were tenacious of life.

In quick stages, he passed from Bangor's stores and poor quarters, through Oldtown, with its remnant of Penobscot Indians, the worse for rum, to the recent clearings of settlers, to the logging camps, and hunters' outposts, until he reached the wilderness. He had with him two woods-wise guides who initiated him into the ways of the forest. His spirits rose as the last traces of human occupation fell behind, and when he reached Katahdin, standing inviolate in its virgin forest, he was elated.

And then a shock. *It was too wild!* The pathless gloom of interlacing evergreens seemed unbearably savage, stern, the home of foreboding. It was ever dreary, desolate, too lost and inhuman to be borne. He felt that his reason was being dispersed and become shadowy, more thin and "subtile, like the air." He felt that Nature was reproaching him for coming there before his time. But she did not completely deprive him of his sense of humor, for he reported, "The summit of Ktaadn had a singularly flat, tableland appearance, like a short highway, where a demigod might be let down to take a turn or two in an afternoon, to settle his dinner."

Henry's description of working his way up the peak takes the reader right along. His prose is as good a vehicle for sight-seers as has been written on this continent. The wild captured him at last and he exclaimed, "What a place to live, what a place to die and be buried in! There certainly men would live forever, and laugh at death and the grave."

Thus he spoke when he let himself go, but he was a realist at heart and forced himself to add, when the party came out of the bush, "Nevertheless, it was a relief to get back to our smooth but still varied landscape."

Henry was twenty-nine on this trip to Katahdin. Seven years later, he took a water trip with an Indian guide into the moose country and was present at the killing of a moose, though "with compunctions." He had accompanied the hunters "as reporter or chaplain," and found that "the afternoon's tragedy, and my share in it, as it affected the innocence, destroyed the pleasure of my adventure." He hated the killing instinct in men who killed more than they needed to support them, for "the sport of it." He was the lover of all nature, so in sympathy with growing things that he could exclaim about the magnificent white pine, "it is the living spirit of the tree, not its spirit of turpentine, with which I sympathize, and which heals my cuts. It is as immortal as I am, and perchance will go to as high a heaven, there to tower above me still."

Henry enjoyed the humor of his Indians and quotes one guide concerning a thunderstorm. "As we lay huddled together under the tent, which leaked considerably about the sides, with our baggage at our feet, we listened to some of the grandest thunder which I ever heard—rapid peals, round and plump, bang, bang, bang, in succession, like artillery from some fortress in the sky; and the lightning was proportionately brilliant. The Indians said, 'It must be good powder.' "

Henry's third and last trip to Maine, when he was forty, carried him through the Allegash and East Branch country. He had a versatile Indian guide, Joe Polis, who had represented his tribe at two capitals, Augusta, Maine, and Washington, D.C. Unlike Henry, he relished New York City. From him the Concord woods-lover learned many an Indian aptitude, although not all—Polis would not divulge his secret way of making the pitch required for canoe repairs. He taught Henry his language, sang religious chants, and confided that he had six thousand dollars in the bank. He would have figured valuably in the book of the Indian which Henry did not live long enough to assemble from his masses of notes.

The Maine Woods, in which accounts of these three excursions appear, was not published until after Henry's death.

He was working on the Allegash account on his deathbed, as Ellery Channing noted in his copy of *The Week,* and the last words that Henry was heard to utter were "moose . . . Indians."

Most motives are mixed, and Henry Thoreau's reasons for erecting a shelter in the quiet of Walden Pond were many. He was glad to be physically active and so dull the memories of his ineffectual efforts in New York and of setting the woods on fire. He craved long periods of uninterrupted hours so that he could get the rivers' trip on paper. He wanted to catch up in his reading and ransack the world of thought. And, above all, he wanted to put his life in perspective and see where it led.

Two years, two months, and two days later, in September, 1847, he grew aware that his idyllic life in its setting of secluded beauty was becoming a temptation. "Perhaps it seemed to me that I had several more lives to live, and could not spare any more time for this one. It is remarkable how easily and insensibly we fall unto a particular route, and make a beaten track for ourselves. Thank Heaven, here is not all the world. The universe is wider than one's views of it."

But how it had paid him to pursue that investigation! "I learned this, at least, by my experiment: that if one advances confidently in the direction of his dreams, and endeavors to live the life which he has imagined, he will meet with a success unexpected in common hours. In proportion as he simplifies his life, the laws of the universe will appear less complex, and solitude will not be solitude, nor poverty poverty, nor weakness weakness. If you have built castles in the air, your work need not be lost; that is where they should be. Now put the foundations under them."

It was time, Henry's conscience told him, to let go of this easy, immensely happy life that he had shared with nature, and put sturdy foundations under his dream hours. Since he was poet and journalist, these foundations would be of words, of true expression. He must write of the life he had divined, life at his own gait, the only gait that would be honest. "If a man does not keep pace with his companions, perhaps it is because he hears a different drummer. Let him keep step to the music which he hears, however measured or far away." "However mean your life is, meet it and live it; do not shun it and call it hard names. It is not so bad as you are. It looks poorest when you are richest." "God will see that you do not want society. It is life near the bone where it is sweetest. You are defended from being a trifler. No man loses ever on a lower level by magnanimity on a higher. Superfluous wealth can buy superfluities only. Money is not required to buy one necessary of the soul. Rather than love, than money, than fame, give me truth."

Henry Thoreau suffered throughout his life from being misunderstood, and opinion of him still is generally unjust. He was human. He wanted love with all the force of his downright nature, although it must be on his own terms. He had to have money to keep himself and, at times, his family alive, and he gave years to the loathed pencil business because his conscience insisted. He had watched Emerson grow to world renown, and, since he knew the worth of his own truth, he wished it could be listened to as widely—which is fame enough for a philosopher.

But truth, its discovery and utterance, came before love,

wealth, or fame. Truth, like the beat of his heart, the circulation of his blood, the processes of his thought, was the prime essential of his conscious being. "There is no truth in him," was the worst one could say about a man. In his two years of arduous reflection, he had garnered enough truth to fill a book. But, as great artists before Henry had discovered, the book should take the form of a story to be accessible to many. The race's truth was dressed up as in *Cinderella* or *The Golden Fleece*. Christian truth was laid out in parables. Bunyan's truth took the shape of *Pilgrim's Progress*. Only now, as wider-eyed readers demanded, the story must *look* wholly true on the surface, and become a sort of detective story in which each interpreter must divine the true meaning for himself.

Henry was artist at heart and he must have enjoyed the prospect of turning his homemade shelter and its woods, stone, and water into a veiled truth-story. Walden Pond should stand, in his book, as a visible sign of the invisible truths he had come upon in his long search. "I thank God that he has made this pond deep and pure for a symbol." He could be thankful also for its coolness, its transparency, its ability to reflect the heaven above, and for being a servant of his desire.

"As I stand over the insect crawling amid the pine needles on the forest floor, and endeavoring to conceal itself from my sight, and ask myself why it will cherish these humble thoughts, and hide its head from me who might, perhaps, be its benefactor, and impart to its race some cheering information, I am reminded of the greater Benefactor and Intelligence that stands over me the human insect."

Everyone has good times and bad, has thoughts of every sort, and so many seemingly disassociated selves that he can hardly discover what he calls *himself*, his bedrock, true self. Since Henry had come to know the great thinkers in the Harvard Library, he had spent his life trying to arrive at his truest self, in action as well as in thought. His Declaration of Independence required just two sentences: "I went to the woods because I wished to live deliberately, to front only the essential facts of life, and see if I could not learn what it had to teach, and not, when I came to die, discover that I had not lived. I did not wish to live what was not life, living is so dear; nor did I wish to practice resignation, unless it was quite necessary."

This program he carried out, and his account of it has become one of the few books which, with pleasant exaggeration, we call "immortal." We elevate it to that rank because it has in its pages so much of the real spiritual life that decay cannot touch it.

What of *Walden* itself? Characteristically, it is compact, meaty, short. The Modern Library edition fits a coat pocket. Edwin Way Teale's beautifully illustrated edition, with the author's photographs of Walden Pond at different seasons, runs to 291 pages, with much factual and enlightening comment prefacing each chapter.

Henry, who was a veritable porcupine with his prickly characteristics, never shed all his quills. Unlike writers who seek to ingratiate themselves with the public by being superficially amiable, Henry resorted to barks to awaken interest.

His first chapter, "Economy," calls names so sharply that the world's hackles rise at the mention of Thoreau. The book starts by comparing the author's way of getting a living with the neighbors' bemused ideas, composed of "unlimited anxiety, strain, and care." He jots down his own expenses, but his was no usual Yankee thrift. His concern is to support one's spiritual life, as well as the body. Nor was his aim to reduce men's existence to his own pondside life, but to make each man consider the spiritual value of what he was paying for. This long, disputatious chapter bristles with debatable pronouncements, unforgettable flashes of wit, and condensations of wisdom in sentences able to withstand the erosion of time. "What a man thinks of himself, that it is which determines, or rather indicates, his fate." "Man's capacities have never been measured; nor are we to judge of what he can do by any precedents, so little has been tried." "I think that we may safely trust a good deal more than we do." "To be a philosopher is not merely to have subtle thoughts, nor even to found a school, but so to love wisdom as to live according to its dictates, a life of simplicity, independence, magnanimity, and trust." "Why has man rooted himself thus firmly in the earth, but that he may rise in the same proportion into the heavens above?" "The life which men praise and regard as successful is but one kind. Why should we exaggerate any one kind at the expense of the others?"

One can quote from this one chapter for pages, but if the tender reader has not yet the stamina for its contentions, he had better start with Chapter 2, "Where I Lived and What I Lived For." This is a hymn to morning joy, to creative leisure. The view from Henry's door was "pasture enough for my imagination." He backed up his delight in the freshness of early day by quoting from the Vedas: "All intelligences awake with the morning. Poetry and art and the fairest and most memorable of the actions of men, date from such an hour. All poets and heroes, like Memnon, are the children of Aurora, and emit their music at sunrise." Even the subway rider hanging to a strap on his way between the twin confinements of his apartment and place of work must get from these thirteen pages a fleeting glimpse of what life is meant to be, according to Henry Thoreau.

He still calls a few names, "We live meanly, like ants," "We are determined to be starved before we are hungry," "Men say that a stitch in time saves nine, and so they take a thousand stitches today to save nine tomorrow. As for *work*, we haven't any of any consequence. We have the Saint Vitus' dance, and cannot possibly keep our heads still."

It is by such barbed generalizations that Henry affronted those who do not agree with what he was after, and pretty well alienated posterity. Yet his admonition to live with less hurry and clutter and thieving detail is still pertinent, and few poets have put the matter more plainly than in his famous sentence, "Time is but the stream I go a-fishing in. I drink at it; but while I drink I see the sandy bottom and detect how shallow it is. Its thin current slides away, but eternity remains."

Surprisingly, *Walden's* third chapter is on "Reading." That was Henry's way of putting foundations under the book. His residence, he said, was more favorable, not only to serious thought, but to serious reading, than a university. Then he tells why he chose the time-tested books. "I think that having

learned our letters we should read the best that is in literature, and not be forever repeating our a-b-abs and words of
one syllable . . . all our lives." Prickle, prickle, but pages of
good sense, and as valuable now as when he was battling in
person against the transient and the pulpy.

"Sounds" is the next subject. While reading, "we are in
danger of forgetting the language which all things and events
speak without metaphor, which alone is copious and standard." Henry, who abounded in metaphors, was blessed with an
eagle's eyesight and a hare's ears. The railroad won him, after
some grumbling and sarcasm, because its whistle sounded like
the scream of a hawk. He capitulated to church bells—at a
distance, and on favorable winds heard the bells of Concord,
Bedford, Lincoln and Acton. Sound was nutriment to him,
whether from a cow under some far horizon or the whippoor-
wills at hand. The screech owl supplied his lullaby, and cock-
crowing delighted him to the point of ecstasy. The last lines
of this lyric chapter preserve the essence of Henry's nature
in one aspect. For him, the outdoor world is charged with
eternal freshness, and its sounds are often vehicles of rapture.

From "Sounds" to the next chapter, "Solitude," was barely
a step, since one was oftenest linked with the other. "This is a
delicious evening, when the whole body is one sense, and
imbibes delight through every pore." There speaks health in
an environment when man and nature merge. "I find it
wholesome to be alone the greater part of the time," as everyone who values his interior life discovers, often too late. One
dines in society and digests in solitude, and if the day is con-
tinuously social, there is no interval for the assimilation which
is the gain desired. "Society is commonly too cheap. We meet

at very short intervals, not having had time to acquire any new value for each other."

This chapter would not be Henry's without some paradoxes. "Why should I feel lonely? is not our planet in the Milky Way?" "I have a great deal of company in my house; especially in the morning, when nobody calls." "I have occasional visits in the long winter evenings, when the snow falls fast and the wind howls in the wood, from an old settler, and original proprietor, who is reported to have dug Walden Pond, and stoned it, and fringed it with pine woods, who tells me stories of old time and of new eternity; and between us we manage to pass a cheerful evening with social mirth and pleasant views of things, even without apples or cider—a most wise and humorous friend, whom I love much, who keeps himself more secret than ever did Goffe or Whalley, and though he is thought to be dead, none can show where he is buried." It is such communication that has given Thoreau a passport to his own immortality.

"Visitors"—children a-berrying, railroad men taking a Sunday morning walk in clean shirts, fishermen, hunters, poets, philosophers, all honest pilgrims who sought the woods for freedom's sake and "really left the village behind"—the one condition that Henry exacted—were welcomed at Walden Lodge, enjoyed, and let depart with equal satisfaction. During the two years of the hermit's sojourn in Concord's green suburb, he probably had more personal company than visited him in his home during his entire life.

"The Bean Field" is the Waldenite at his observant best. His two and one-half acres of beans were so near the road that he heard comments not meant for his ear: "Beans so late!

Peas so late!" and "Does he *live* there?" His expenses came to
$14.72½, his returns, $23.44; but, in addition to his summer
food, he had a lasting satisfaction in making the earth say
"beans," and he raised crops of health, philosophy, and pure
happiness. The next year, though, he planted only half an
acre.

"The Village" figures next, and complements the picture
of himself outlined in "Solitude." One cannot tell the unin-
formed too often that Henry visited Concord nearly every
day, and enjoyed the village gossip "which, taken in homeo-
pathic doses, was really as refreshing in its way as the rustle of
leaves and the peeping of frogs." It is a short chapter, however, followed by "The Ponds," with Henry's celebrated account of his surroundings in a prose so cleansed of verbal
impurities and excesses that it has the transparency of the
waters it describes. To quote Edwin Way Teale, "Walden
Pond is so real and so important in the eyes of far-off readers
that, according to the story, an Australian schoolboy named
as 'the three most important bodies of water in the United
States' the Great Lakes, the Mississippi River, and Walden
Pond."

"Baker Farm" was often an object of Henry's rambles. He
tells of being routed by a thunderstorm and writes, "the gods
must be proud, thought I, with such forked flashes to rout a
poor unarmed fisherman." He runs into an Irishman named
John Field, and there follows such a warm amusing description as to make us wish that Henry had written at least one
novel.

"Higher Laws" treats of a man's duty to listen to the
"faintest but constant suggestions of his genius," so that he

will never be misled. "Our whole life is startlingly moral. There is never an instant's truce between virtue and vice. Goodness is the only investment that never fails." He talks of purity and sensuality, "Every man is the builder of a temple, called his body, to the god he worships, after a style purely his own, nor can he get off by hammering marble instead. We are all sculptors and painters, and our material is our own flesh and blood and bones. Any nobleness begins at once to refine a man's features, and any meanness or sensuality to imbrute them."

"Brute Neighbors" starts with a dialogue between *Hermit*, who was Henry, and *Poet*, his friend, the rather sparrow-witted Channing. Henry employs this light talk as a ladder to let the reader down from "Higher Laws" to a description of the small fry about his cabin.

"House Warming" reverts to his first October at Walden Pond, his chimney-building and talk of guests and the coming of winter. "Every man looks at his wood-pile with a kind of affection." That wood warmed him twice, when he was splitting it and when he burned it. For economy's sake, he used a small cooking-stove during his second winter. But "it concealed the fire, and I felt that I had lost a companion. You can always see a face in the fire."

"Former Inhabitants and Winter Visitors" celebrates the time of deep snows and reflection on eternal matters. Herein he etches a portrait of a soldier of Waterloo and pays a tribute to Channing, writing, "The one who came from farthest to my lodge through deepest snows and most dismal tempests, was a poet. A farmer, a hunter, a soldier, a reporter, even a philosopher, may be daunted; but nothing can deter a poet, for he is actuated by pure love. Who can predict his comings and goings? His business calls him out at all hours, even when doctors sleep. We made that small house ring with boisterous mirth and resound with the murmur of much sober talk."

"Winter Animals" and "The Ponds in Winter" round out the picture and bring us to "Spring" and Henry's joy in returning life. He turns even the thaw into poetry. He felt that he "stood in the laboratory of the Artist who made the world and me." He realized from every phase of nature, the procession of the day from morning through noon to night, the progress of the year, the life of trees and flowers and rocks, that "There is nothing inorganic"—dead stuff—but living poetry, and he recognized that "the intellect is a cleaver; it discerns and rifts its way into the secret of things."

Through intuition, reinforced by observation, he reached the conclusion of modern science, and Wernher von Braun can now say, "I believe in an immortal soul. Science has proved that nothing disintegrates into nothingness. Life and soul, therefore, cannot disintegrate into nothingness, and so are immortal."

In a typically Thoreauvian sentence, Henry declares that God "is a very *present* help in trouble, but the chief trouble is that we live in the past and in tradition, where he is not."

Chapter 18, "Conclusion," contains a wonderful parable concerning the obligations and rewards of the eternal present. It ends in famous words that have been quoted ever since, "The light which puts out our eyes is darkness to us. Only that day dawns to which we are awake. There is more day to dawn. The sun is but a morning star."

These words bear thinking about for the rest of one's life.

172

TEN

Henry vs. the Times

ON Monday, September 6, 1847, Henry Thoreau ousted himself from his private Garden of Eden and rejoined society in its own haunts, for several reasons. He wished to push the publication of *A Week on the Concord and Merrimack Rivers.* His Journal was rich in material for his next book, *Walden.* Emerson was going to England in October, and Lidian had invited Henry to man the house during her husband's absence. The children were overjoyed when he accepted.

One can imagine the poignant feelings when the tenant of Paradise realized that his term was over. His snug house was left to the mouse and the wasps who had been used to sharing Henry's bed with him as autumn came on and forbore to sting him. Emerson's gardener moved the hut to the bean field presently, but got drunk and ran away, and Thoreau finally planted pines in the bean field.

Henry found himself surprisingly busy in Emerson's home, for Lidian was in poor health and he helped run the house. His letters to Emerson were high-spirited, often amusing, reports of affairs. But four publishers rejected the *Week.* On Emerson's advice, Henry contracted with James Munroe, the Boston printer and bookseller, to pay for its publication. Following unexplained delays, the book appeared in May, 1849, after lying for ten years on Henry's mind and heart.

Bronson Alcott was enthusiastic about it, calling it "an American book, worthy to stand beside Emerson's essays." A review in the New York *Tribune* praised it as "A really new book—a fresh, original thoughtful work." In England, the historian Froude wrote to Henry, "In your book . . . I see hope for the coming world." James Russell Lowell, who rarely found anything to praise in Henry, published a long, appreciative survey of the book in the *Massachusetts Quarterly Review*. This delighted the Thoreau family, and Aunt Maria wrote of the *Week* as being "so just and pleasant, and some parts of it so laughable."

The booksellers might as well have been trying to sell white elephants, however. Henry had paid to have a thousand copies printed. In four years, only 294 copies had been disposed of. James Munroe asked Henry to rid his cellar of the 706 copies remaining. So the author sent for them and wrote in his Journal with grim humor, "The wares are sent to me at last, and I have an opportunity to examine my purchase. They are something more substantial than fame, as my back knows, which has borne them up two flights of stairs to a place similar to that to which they trace their origin. Of the remaining two hundred and ninety and odd, seventy-five were given away, the rest sold. I have now a library of nearly nine hundred volumes, over seven hundred of which I wrote myself."

It is a wisely brave man who can joke in the face of misfortune, and Henry was as brave as a warrior for the right should be. Fortunately, he was blessed with a wry humor that never lost confidence in itself and made jokes that stay fresh forever. His pages are as rich in mirth as Concord's soil with the arrowheads which resemble his humor in texture and pointedness.

The *Week* is still good reading. Henry knew the poet's rule, that it is the particulars which point out the wholes. His pages carry both physical facts and spiritual findings. The facts interest because they are so freshly observed; the findings are thrilling because they connect the seen with the invisible. Henry had already learned how to glean the best of both worlds, and, like Bunyan's Pilgrim, he was making a dual journey, on the earth and above the sky.

The dull booksellers and the obtuse public made the *Week* seem a failure, utterly unimportant to an American which was violently alive. Gold had been discovered in California. Slavery was searing the conscience of the North. The Missouri Compromise and the Fugitive Slave Law had created an uproar that drowned out Henry's quiet voice. A long book about an undangerous trip through a familiar countryside had no chance at such a moment, and this was a severe blow to Henry, who had hoped to finance his account of the Walden Pond experiment from its sales.

The failure of the *Week* left him with a debt to pay off at a time when his family also needed money, so he assisted with the pencil-making, worked as a surveyor, and fought off ill health. The harmony of the Walden years had kept him free from colds; now he was threatened with the family curse, tuberculosis. His sister died of that disease before his anguished eyes. His father was to die of it, as was he, in a few years. Fortunately, while writing *Walden*, he lived over again in his mind and spirit that time of great, though quiet, joy. He finished the book in the stillness of mourning for

Helen and kept death out of it. Then began the long struggle with obtuse publishers who unanimously decided not to tie up their funds in such a contentious book.

Henry's family did not wish it published, either, unless Henry would delete passages which seemed to them sacrilegious. This the embattled author would not do. One can imagine the strain on home-loving Henry. His surest, deepest, most impassioned convictions had gone into this work. Was love's labor to be watered down into a sort of skimmed milk of the word to please his relatives? Was he to go back on his own religion to make peace with people who loved but often misunderstood him?

Aunt Maria's letter to Prudence Ward in 1849 anticipated the answer. She says of Henry ". . . he is preparing his Book for the press and the title is to be, Waldien (I dont know how to spell it) or Life in the Woods. I think the title will take if the Book dont . . . and Henry is putting things into his Book that never ought to be there . . . you know I have said, there were parts of it that sounded to me very much like blasphemy, and I did not believe they would publish it, or reading it to Helen the other day Sophia told me, she made the same remark, and coming from her, Henry was much surprised, and said she did not understand it, but still I fear they will not persuade him to leave it out."

The garrulous and ungrammatical Aunt Maria at least knew her nephew that well. Henry's bottommost principle was integrity. He could not mutilate thoughts that he believed to be true because his womenfolk wanted him to. He considered that a man, to be *himself*, to be eternally the individual he was created to be, should hunt for his true point of view until he was assured, deep within, that he had found it. Here is his declaration on that point:

> Do not speak for other men; speak for yourself. Though you should only speak to one kindred mind in all time, though you should not speak to one, but only utter aloud, that you may the more completely realize and live in the idea, which contains the reason of your life, that you may build yourself up to the height of your conceptions, that you may remember your Creator in the days of your youth and justify His ways to man, that the end of life may not be its amusement, speak—though your thought presupposes the nonexistence of your hearers—thoughts that transcend life and death.

That wilderness of a sentence has to be entered carefully, traversed phrase by phrase slowly, and the trail retraced often; but it brings the faithful tracker out on the glory of existence. It may not save one from error, but it can keep him from committing infidelity to his immortal soul. And Henry followed his own precept so closely and courageously that Fame, exclusive as she is, had to recognize him at last.

It had taken all of Henry's living to lead up to the vision of that one-sentence pronouncement. When he had hinted this boldness in his Harvard papers, he was called bumptious. It cast its light ahead in his lectures, "Life without Principle" and "Civil Disobedience." Now it was going to require all his character to face his share of the great struggle between slave-keeping and emancipation.

Henry was so outraged by the Fugitive Slave Law that he

delighted in breaking it when opportunity offered. One day when Louisa May Alcott was helping him in the garden, she saw one flowering weed so lovely that she hated to pull it up. "Do I have to, Mr. Thoreau?" she asked.

He came to her. "Certainly not. Weeds were here first and have squatters' rights. A divinity stirs within them as surely as in roses. Only a divinity could enable a plant that roots in darkness to blossom in stars."

"Excuse me, Mr. Thoreau." A young man approached. "May I speak to you alone?"

Louisa May withdrew and the man said, "The ship, *Northern Star,* has been raided by slave-catchers. We had twenty-one fugitives aboard. They jumped into the water. We pulled eight out, two drowned, the rest were recaptured. The eight should reach Concord about ten o'clock tonight, in the Marshalls' freight van. They must be hidden until we can arrange for transportation north."

"Eight," Henry said dubiously. "A problem. More than once we have secreted a runaway slave in our cellar—but eight! For how long this time?"

"We should have them off in twenty-four hours. The slave-catchers have lively leaders and won't stop at bloodshed. High rewards are offered. Since the Evanses were prosecuted for hiding that Georgia slave, people are wary of helping."

"Yes, to be guilty of mercy is now as dangerous as murder!" Henry's voice was hard. "To such a pass has greed brought us. I'll have arrangements made by suppertime, friend. Come after dark."

The trouble was that Mr. Brooks, who managed these undertakings, was in Boston, and his sister, who cooked for the fugitives, was ill. Henry could not ask his mother, who might let the cat out of the bag in an unguarded moment and endanger *eight* lives—too many to risk. Then, as Louisa May rejoined him, the plan came to him. His old hut on the bean field would shelter eight, and Louisa could cook. Bronson Alcott would be glad to let her help. They could hang blankets over the windows.

It was nearly midnight by the stars when Henry heard the sound of heavy wheels nearing. He struck a match; blew it out. The van pulled into the bean field. Dark, silent figures slid out of the van and lay on the ground, almost too worn and stiff to move. The driver said in a low tone, "Be in your garden at sundown tomorrow. I'll have news." The van crunched its way out to the road, and when silence gathered about them, Henry guided the silent men to the shelter.

The night was warm and still. The fugitives sat on the pondward side of the cabin, holding the bowls of soup that Louisa and her mother had readied. When the girl refilled the bowls, the Negroes mumbled, "Thank you, Missy." "I'se much obleeged, ma'am." "God bress you, Miss."

The next round of food was a platter of cold pork, corn-cakes, molasses. Sympathizers had given money in small amounts and lent blankets. Henry thought it safe for the men to sleep outdoors until sunrise.

"God look after you-all for this," an old Negro woman said to Mrs. Alcott.

"Ah don' know enuf ways to say thank you, ma'am," said another.

"Why is de white folks up No'th so diffrunt from ours?" a young man asked.

Their gratitude worked on Louisa May's feelings and she said to Henry, "They thank me for doing what we'd do for a stray dog. How wicked to bring good people so low!"

As dawn neared, the Alcotts went home, to return after dark, and the fugitives packed themselves in the hut. There was one more than the floor would accommodate easily, and Henry took him to a hiding place in the woods. They had a long talk and the man explained how he had made his way north after escaping from the plantation. He guided himself by the north star. "Dat one, ah kin trust. De udders skim aroun', but not him." He also had followed the telegraph wire, and the sun did its part in steering him.

A drenching rain cooled the afternoon, and left a helpful mist. The fugitives, long used to misery, made light of the long wait, and devoured the evening meal with embarrassing gratitude. When the van reappeared, the fugitives surrounded Henry to whisper their thanks and press his hand, then were swallowed up in the rescuing blackness.

Henry went back to the hut to destroy all evidence of use; it could be used again. He was exhausted but happy. It pleased him to have this new tie with the Alcotts, his accomplices now, subject to fines and imprisonment—for doing good. Surely some awful retribution must come to the land for this long-continued sin.

Henry had so many ties with the slaves' Promised Land, Canada, that he wanted to see it. He had already visited Cape Cod alone and with Ellery Channing, and he suggested to Channing that they visit French Canada at least. This they did, and Henry made a book of his notes, *A Yankee in Canada.* It revealed to him how satisfactory the United States was, in spite of its slaveholders and money-grabbers. He hunted down the sights, like any tourist, made no great effort to penetrate to the hearts of these descendants of the feudal system, and was guilty of unbecoming remarks about their religion.

He was amused by the Highlanders in their kilts and said, "If you wish to study the muscles of the leg about the knee, repair to Quebec." He stared at the fortifications of Quebec so steadily that he was afraid of becoming "wall-eyed." He was captivated by the great river, the St. Lawrence, whose history is as notable as its climate, geography, and meaning to Canada. But even a Thoreau, well-read and a trained observer, could observe little in a trip of twelve and one half days. *A Yankee in Canada* is the least important of his travel books, but entertaining because of the keen eye and light touch with which Henry dispensed his opinions.

Four visits to Cape Cod insured a greater richness to that book. Here he had the ocean as assistant and American history for background. It thrilled him that "the nearest beach on the other side was on the coast of Galicia, in Spain." Also, he stumbled on drama only two days after the wrecking of the brig *St. John,* from Galway, laden with emigrants. He was both realist and poet, and describes vividly the hopeless confusion of wreckage and drowned bodies, with the seekers trying to identify relatives, and ever the sea's dirge heard in "the pure and unqualified strain of eternal memory."

His pictorial and amusing interview with the Wellfleet oysterman reminds one again of the tremendous reporter

New York lost when it cold-shouldered young Henry Thoreau a dozen years earlier. He puts down the man's talk so accurately that one can see his "grizzly-looking" appearance and hear his toothless voice.

" 'These women,' said he to me, 'are both of them poor good-for-nothing critturs. This one is my wife. I married her sixty-four years ago. She is eighty-four years old, and as deaf as an adder, and the other is not much better.' " The other was his daughter.

"He thought well of the Bible, or at least *spoke* well, and did not *think* ill, of it, for that would not have been prudent for a man of his age. He seemed deeply impressed with a sense of his own nothingness, and would repeatedly exclaim, 'I am a nothing. What I gather from my Bible is just this: that man is a poor good-for-nothing crittur, and everything is just as God sees fit and disposes.'

" 'May I ask your name?' I said.

" 'Yes,' he answered. 'I am not ashamed to tell my name.' "

Henry goes on to ferret out the truth about oysters in this interview, which would have built a reputation for him if it had been part of a novel. The whole book seems as alive as when he set it down. In it he is naturalist first, giving a realistic accounting of all he encounters, the humanity, the humor, the strangeness of that life so involved in the sea. He enjoyed singing "Tom Bowling," danced with pleasure, responded to friendly advances—unless they cut across his way of life. *Cape Cod* lives still because he put so much life into it.

Henry shared Emerson's view that travel was a fool's paradise, although both men traveled extensively and were no fools. Henry wrote to his friend, Harrison Blake, "Where is the 'unexplored land' but in our own untried enterprises? To an adventurous spirit any place—London, New York, Worcester, or his own back yard—is 'unexplored land.' These are the regions of the Known and the Unknown. You must make tracks into the Unknown."

Yet Henry's explorations in Maine, Canada, and on Cape Cod added to his tangible experience, and his thought had wider tried horizons. His meeting with the ocean was particularly releasing. He was learning on his excursions that the denominator he had in common with all men was greater than he had suspected.

The times helped to stretch his sympathies. Slavery was now the universal topic, and abolition filled the air that Henry breathed. The women in his home read Garrison's paper, *The Liberator,* aloud to each other, and young Frank Sanborn, who was taking his meals at the Thoreau table and who admired Henry so much that he wrote a life of him, was influenced to the point of befriending John Brown of the Harper's Ferry raid.

Henry hated all slavery, including the slavery to money and things which one did not have to go South to find. He summed up his feelings in one sentence, "It is hard to have a Southern overseer; it is worse to have a Northern one; but worst of all when you are yourself the slave-driver." He wondered that men were wrought up only by the Southern sort of slavery, when there were so many keen and subtle masters who subjected men to their whip. Henry advocated self-emancipation of one's thinking. It would knock off the fetters from a million slaves—Northern variety.

Presently, Henry's feelings were set afire by the Burns case—a Negro had been sent back to the slavers in a vessel provided by the government. Henry said that he had been listening for the voice of the Governor in expostulation and heard—only the crickets. His walks, his day, were overcast by this cowardly assistance to injustice. "My thoughts were murder to the State," he said in a line worthy of Shakespeare.

So he wrote an address and gave it, significantly on Independence Day, 1854, at Framingham, near Concord, with the biting title, "Slavery in Massachusetts." His sentences rang with an indignation buttressed by universal truth. "I wish my countrymen to consider that, whatever the human law may be, neither an individual nor a nation can ever commit the least act of injustice against the obscurest individual without having to pay the penalty for it." Henry had learned the Law of Compensation well.

He went on, "I have lived for the last month—and I think every man in Massachusetts capable of the sentiment of patriotism must have had a similar experience—with the sense of having suffered a vast and indefinite loss. I did not know at first what ailed me. At last it occurred to me that what I had lost was a country."

"We have used up all our inherited freedom. If we would save our lives, we must fight for them."

Here was a new side of Henry Thoreau, revealed under stress. In New York, the *Tribune* summarized the speech at length and said that Thoreau rather than Sumner or Seward should be called the real champion of a "Higher Law."

The saunterer through the woods and river-lover had indeed taken on new stature. He lectured on "Life without Principle." His point was that, if you work at something your heart is not in, you cheat yourself and are being paid for being something less than a man. "You must get your living by loving," that is, choose a work you can perform with all your heart. If the world attended to this principle, the result would be not slaves, not operatives, but men, "those rare fruits called heroes, saints, poets, philosophers and redeemers."

Henry was speaking with the whole force of his life to back him up. His intensity of conviction led him into making statements so extreme that they boomeranged on him. But there was so much truth in his words that they are just as living and needed today as a century ago. He sought to be a man of principle himself and looked for his friends among men of principle. Presently, he found a man he deemed of like character, although history has qualified his judgment considerably. The man's name was John Brown of Osawatomie.

He was the most hated man in Kansas, whose territory he had striven to keep free. He had enlisted his sons to fight the Border Ruffians and had killed twenty-five men himself. He had come East on a fund-raising expedition, and one can imagine the talk in the Thoreau home, as the women listened to so strange a guest. Henry, the uncompromising idealist, condoned violence under Brown's influence and complained only that the agitator would not communicate his plans.

Two years later, John Brown returned and spoke in Concord's Town Hall, still keeping his plans to himself. Then came the raid at Harper's Ferry, the reckless effort to overthrow slavery, no matter what the cost in blood. Brown's arrest, that October of 1859, hit Henry where he was most sensitive. He poured out his heart in his Journal, 10,000 words in three days. His incendiary language was the second Concord fire, and meant to spread, but the whole country, including northern Republicans and stanch Abolitionists, condemned Henry's hero. With Brown awaiting execution, Henry summoned Concord to listen to his plea for the doomed man.

This act, however mistaken, was the bravest deed of Henry's brave life. Concord abhorred Brown and was incensed at Henry, who had so often affronted its feelings. This time, Henry was pleading less for the doomed man than for principle. "It costs us nothing to be just," he began. His address was incandescent with his fiery mood. Hindsight has convinced us that he was wrong, but he did not have hindsight's perspective. What concerns this account is *Henry's* act, his courage at facing a possible tarring and feathering at the mob's hands for standing up for his convictions.

Henry Canby has called "A Plea for John Brown," one of the great public addresses in American history, and it was Henry's finest hour, in the sense that he burned then with his purest and intensest flame. Emerson recorded that the address was delivered with such passion and eloquence that it was "heard by all respectfully, by many with a sympathy that surprised themselves." As Canby says, Henry's "minority of one soon increased to the million of which he spoke." Thus does the innate virtue of a man emerge in crisis.

ELEVEN

The Summing-Up

IN 1855, when Henry was thirty-eight, he suffered a long illness and, during the slow hours of convalescence, he meditated on the master plan which was to occupy his mind for the rest of his life.

His youthful ecstasy in nature had sobered somewhat, but his past experiences had stored up "a never-failing capital. Our stock in life, our real estate, is that amount of thought which we have had, which we have thought out. The ground we have thus created is forever pasturage for our thoughts. I fall back on to visions which I have had."

This master plan was a history of Concord, from Indian times to his own, complete with nature's *Kalendar*, as he spelled it. He had been recording the progress of the seasons, for the joy they brought. Now he would measure them with all the instruments at hand, from magnifying glass to telescope. His Journal became less a poet's handbook and more a scientific repository.

The *Kalendar* was to be all-inclusive, and some of its chapters had been written, "Autumnal Tints," "November Lights," "The Succession of Forest Trees." Henry's learning enabled him to draw from the wisest observers of our race, from Aristotle to Agassiz. He had outgrown the confines of his ego and could say, "It is the spirit of humanity, that which animates so-called savages and civilized nations, working through a man, and not the man expressing himself, that interests us most."

In spite of the seeds of tuberculosis in him, Henry found energy for varied endeavors. After his father's death in 1859, he took on the entire responsibility for his family's welfare. The sale of graphite had proven more lucrative than marketing lead pencils, and he derived some income from surveying until 1860. He also paid more attention to friends beyond the boundaries of Concord.

Harrison Blake was possibly his closest friend, to judge by the frankness of Henry's letters to this lifelong admirer who lived in Worcester. Daniel Ricketson, of New Bedford, established a rather one-sided friendship with Henry. He continually invited the Concord stay-at-home to be his guest and was just as often put off with replies like this, "Such are my engagements to myself, that I dare not promise to wend your way." Ricketson was at last allowed to walk with Henry and Emerson on the cliffs of Fair Haven. He would talk of life's sufferings until Henry cut him short with, "No ecstasy was ever interrupted, nor its fruit blasted. We want no completeness but intensity of life." That was the artist in Henry staking out his claim.

Bronson Alcott persuaded Henry to return to New York to see Walt Whitman, whose *Leaves of Grass* had kicked up controversy since its publication in 1855. Alcott's description of the two men is amusing: "Planted fast in reserves, surveying the other curiously—like two beasts, each wondering what the other would do, whether to snap or run, and it came to no more than cold compliments between them."

Henry wrote to Blake about Whitman, "He is apparently the greatest democrat the world has seen. Kings and aristocracy go by the board at once, as they have long deserved to. A remarkably strong though coarse nature, of a sweet disposition, and much prized by his friends."

Whitman had sized up Henry, too. "Thoreau had his own odd ways. Once he got to the house while I was out—went straight to the kitchen where my dear mother was baking cakes—took the cakes hot from the oven. He was always doing things of the plain sort—without fuss. I liked all that about him. But Thoreau's great fault was disdain—disdain for men (for Tom, Dick, and Harry); inability to appreciate the average life—even the exceptional life; it seemed to me a want of imagination. He couldn't put his life into any other life—realize why one man was so and another man was not so; was impatient with other people on the street, and so forth."

It is hard to know another individual well, and impossible to know him completely. When the individuals concerned are geniuses, as Whitman and Thoreau were, the exploration of each other is more difficult still. Whitman loved cities and people *en masse;* Henry loved nature and persons one at a time. He loved man so deeply that when men took themselves cheaply, throwing away life on inessentials, he grew angry. He called such wasters hard names, yet it would be difficult to find in American history anyone who hoped more for man and cared more passionately for his well-being than Henry David Thoreau.

He disliked politics, and when the guns of Fort Sumter echoed through his woods, he wrote, "Blessed are they who never read a newspaper, for they shall see Nature, and through her, God." He wished to save the Union, but was far more anxious to preserve man's personal integrity. The North's defeat at Bull Run was a personal blow, so severe that he told Sophia that he would never get well until the war was ended, not then knowing that the war would outlast him by three years.

Henry wrote a rich autumnal essay, "Walking." By that activity he meant sauntering, observing, enjoying, gathering thoughts when ripe, as he gathered huckleberries. He wrote, "I have met with but one or two persons in the course of my life who understood the art of Walking, that is, of taking walks—who had a genius, so to speak, for *sauntering*: which word is beautifully derived 'from idle people who roved about the country, in the Middle Ages, and asked charity, under pretense of going à la Sainte Terre,' to the Holy Land, till the children exclaimed, 'There goes a Sainte Terrer,' a Saunterer, a Holy-Lander."

He went on to say, "I think I cannot preserve my health or spirits unless I spend four hours a day at least—and it is commonly more than that—sauntering through the woods and over the hills and fields, absolutely free from all worldly engagements."

Here are some of the reflections gathered up in that pail of his, the Journal, and transcribed in the essay, which was first a lecture at Amherst:

"If you would get exercise, go in search of the springs of life."

"Moreover, you must walk like a camel, which is said to be the only beast which ruminates while walking."

THE SUMMING-UP

"I am alarmed when it happens that I have walked a mile into the woods bodily, without getting there in spirit."

"In literature it is only the wild that attracts us. Dullness is but another name for tameness. It is the uncivilized free and wild thinking in *Hamlet* and the *Iliad*, in all the Scriptures and Mythologies, not learned in the schools, that delights us." He mentions a strain of music as emblematic of all wildness.

"It is not the part of a true culture to tame tigers, any more than it is to make sheep ferocious."

"I would not have every man or every part of a man cultivated, any more than I would have every acre of earth cultivated."

Henry Thoreau could not help but suspect now that he was soon to die. "So we saunter toward the Holy Land, till one day the sun shall shine more brightly than ever he has done, shall perchance shine into our minds and hearts, and light up our whole lives with a great awakening light, as warm and serene and golden as on a bankside in autumn."

Henry traveled to Minnesota in the hope that its climate might arrest his disease, but its ravagings had gone too far. He had never considered rain water inimical to him, and caught his final cold from kneeling in the slush of a miserable day to count the rings of a fallen tree. Yet his illness was as prolonged as a northern sunset and in a way as beautiful. Death he had long before accepted as natural and inevitable in the sequence called life, as night followed morning, and winter summer. "It is better some things should end," he told Channing.

Happily, he was living out these days of diminishing

strength in his home, with Cynthia and Sophia attending to his wants. He worked to put his lectures and excursions into printable shape. He hoped to arrange for a new edition of the *Week,* but often could not conquer the feebleness that afflicted his body. He coughed much and his voice sank to a whisper. The children, his lifelong friends, brought him flowers, and older visitors looked in. His mind was able to polish his thoughts into a diamond brilliance which makes them still quotable. When pious Aunt Eliza asked if he had made his peace with God, Henry replied that he had never quarreled with Him. Another visitor had the temerity to investigate his views of the hereafter, and Henry retorted, "One world at a time."

Henry's jailer, fellow surveyor and friend, Sam Staples, reported to Emerson his last visit with Thoreau and said, "Never spent an hour with more satisfaction. Never saw a man dying with so much pleasure and peace."

Finally, at nine in the morning of May 6, 1862, the family noticed the invalid's signal to be lifted up. They gently held him upright on the narrow rattan day bed which he had made himself, and his spirit passed away imperceptibly, without sign of struggle or pain. Henry always had preferred the morning for his excursions.

By the desire of his home town, which had been so long in coming to appreciate his worth, a public funeral was held for Henry in the Parish Church—a triple irony for the man who avoided publicity, society, and church buildings. Bronson Alcott read that early poem of Henry's, *Sic Vita,* beginning,

I am a parcel of vain longings tied
By a chance bond together—

a poem of boyhood's indecisions, all over now. Then Emerson read "with broken, tender voice" his moving tribute to this fellow interpreter of life, whom he had so often befriended. Henry's irritations were passed over and forgiven at last in these beautiful paragraphs, the last lines rising to a stirring and prophetic eloquence:

> The country knows not yet, or in the least part, how great a son it has lost. It seems an injury that he should leave in the midst his broken task which none else can finish, a kind of indignity to so noble a soul that he should depart out of Nature before yet he has been really shown to his peers for what he is. But he, at least, is content. His soul was made for the noblest society; he had in a short life exhausted the capabilities of this world; wherever there is knowledge, wherever there is virtue, wherever there is beauty, he will find a home.

For once, "burnt woods" was not called after him, as his body was borne through the streets he had trod a thousand times before Concord was awake, and up to the burial ground so exquisitely called Sleepy Hollow that he himself might have named it. Appropriately, a large rock was reared as his headstone, and in death he was to be surrounded by the friends of his life: Cynthia and Sophia, his father and the one he loved most of all, his brother John, and eventually Lidian and Ralph Waldo Emerson.

What was left to remember when the mourners went home?

There began to take shape the outlines of a courageous man of principle, capable of anger at the follies of his fellows who, he felt, followed the paths of least resistance, to their spiritual crippling. A man who found solace in every aspect of nature from the hop-toad to the heavens, where the constellations were permanent reminders of the universal Presence. A man whose desire for himself, his neighbors and the world beyond, was to take the decisive step from things to spirit. A man who wrote "Love is a thirst that is never slaked," who adhered to his intuitions, to the spiritual necessities of his being, even when it meant separation from the persons who had stirred that love, one who could say to his closest companions, "Farewell, my friends, my path inclines to this side the mountain, yours to that."

The mourners had reminders on every side that this never-pretending Concordian was utterly devoid of hypocrisy and untruth. By a man's loves one can know him, if not entirely, and Henry's love began at home with his familly and lasted without break, and was realized in the upper room, where he released his feelings in rhyme or sculptured his meditations into sentences so long tempered in the heat of his mind that time could not wear them away.

These mourners became conscious of having known a truly good man, whose irritating faults came not from defile-ment of character but from an excess of well-wishing for others. They could not know him in his ecstasies, which were more private in him than in most and cannot be divulged in words, even Shakespeare's words. They could barely guess the intensity of his love for the wild, for the solitude it offered, and the music that his own life created in him.

They might visit in vain the ancient glacial bowls back of Revolutionary Ridge, where the thrushes came in May, and which he called Thrush Alley. He never brought anyone to the evening concerts of thrush song because the music was composed in the key of solitude where two is a crowd.

His own song reached its heights in his recording of his feeling when an invisible company of thrushes praised the primeval beauty while the shadows deepened, and the pines, that had turned the winds of a century into an old hymn, stood by the little ponds in somber majesty.

No wonder that Henry thought, "This is the gospel according to the wood thrush. He makes a sabbath out of a week-day." And, "There is all the romance of my youthfulest moment in music. Heaven lies about us, as in our infancy. There is nothing so wild and extravagant that it does not make true. It makes a dream my only real experience, and prompts faith to such elasticity that only the incredible can satisfy it. It tells me again to trust the remotest and finest, as the divinest, instinct. All that I have imagined of heroism, it reminds and assures me of. It is a life unlived, a life beyond life, where at length my years will pass. I look under the lids of Time."

He spoke of the thrush's music as "cool bars of melody from the atmosphere of everlasting morning or evening. . . . Whenever a man hears it, he is young, and Nature is in her spring. Wherever he hears it, it is a new world and a free country, and the gates of heaven are not shut against him."

Genius, in Henry's case, was not only the "infinite capacity for taking pains," as in his rewritings, but also the infinite capacity for receiving joy. His genius was ecstasy founded upon fact. It was the recognition and employment of his true being in the landscape of daily life, now sunny in happiness, now cloud-shadowed with grief. His genius might weep for others, never for himself.

Just as paradox is the final refuge of truth, so Henry, in his truth, seemed paradoxical: American and village-born, yet universal; the completest idler, yet waster of no hour; a man profoundly serious while a master of humor; a defender of wildness and friend of true civilization; the freest man imaginable and most sensitive to the rights of love.

Genius has visited this earth in many guises; but since it is the advance guard of a subtler civilization, it is rarely recognized fully in its time. It is first noted because of its impossible heights, which discourage the overoccupied mass of men. Half of Henry's thought was devoted to scaling those heights, especially those of love and of friendship. His demands were insatiable. "I have never met with a friend who furnished me sea-room. I have only tacked a few times and come to anchor—not sailed—made no voyage, carried no venture." He explored the upper reaches of friendship's continent and was cried down as mad because he ventured above the snow line of other men's experience.

Once, when he was first lost in the new land of love, he left this message to guide others exploring the same wilderness—"There is no remedy for love but to love more," and farther on, "There is nothing so stable and unfluctuating as love." Many who have come after him and found these signposts have thanked him in their hearts.

Henry's Journals, some two million words long, the work

of a quarter of a century, are his enduring monument—the biography of his heart, mind, and spirit, and a revelation of the unfolding of his being as it was taking place. Occasionally, we let these volumes go out of print, saying as usual, "they do not pay," but always some farther-seeing publisher brings them back to a world that never needed them more than now.

Henry knew that it was the final wording of a thought that made a page immortal, so he spent himself in the working-over of a thought until it reached a verbal perfection that gave it a chance to stand above the flood, the daily Mississippi of thoughts uttered by the million. He left some hints about the process of improving one's writing: "Nothing goes by luck in composition. It allows of no tricks. The best you can write will be the best you are. Every sentence is the result of a long probation. The author's character is read from the title-page to the end. Of this he never corrects the proofs."

"I can express adequately only the thought which I *love* to express."

"Do nothing out of good resolutions. Discipline yourself only to yield to love; suffer yourself to be attracted. It is in vain to write on chosen themes. We must wait until they have kindled a flame in our minds. . . . The theme seeks me, not I it. The poet's relation to this theme is the relation of lovers."

"By the quality of a man's writing, by the elevation of its tone, you may measure his self-respect."

It is as good a test as any.

HENRY THOREAU: AMERICAN REBEL

In the roll call of illustrious American writers, Irving and Cooper, Emerson and Hawthorne, Melville and Whitman and Poe and Twain, Henry Thoreau usually comes last to mind. Nor was it his country's fault that he was so little known when he died in the furore of the Civil War's second year. Only the *Week* and *Walden* had seen print. Later, *Cape Cod, The Maine Woods,* and *A Yankee in Canada* reached a very limited public. Harrison Blake may probably have supplied the turn of the tide when he pasted together the first organized anthology of the Journals in the volumes entitled *Early Spring in Massachusetts, Summer, Winter,* and *Autumn.* But he left out the heart of Thoreau, since he emphasized Henry's interest in nature and, as a result, the public came to think of the man as a naturalist only.

Yet the last may be first, after all. While those other worthies are aging a little and are being treated as literary history, Thoreau becomes more timely all the while. He stressed the fundamental health of an outgoing love, and that is now seen as our greatest need. He insisted that man drop the inessential and seek the essential, and this has become all the more necessary in our crowded life. He gloried in freedom, in his personal independence, and we strive for just that. And, above all, he was the foe of injustice, and our great struggle today is for justice to all, human rights for all. Also, he became a great prose artist. His dawn has arrived and his full day will follow.

Bibliography

IF I were advising young people as to what to read in order to become acquainted with our great writer Thoreau, I should say:

Walden, in Edwin Way Teale's illustrated edition published by Dodd, Mead.

A Week on the Concord and Merrimack Rivers.

Cape Cod.

The Maine Woods.

Shortened versions of these three books are found in The Modern Library edition of *Walden and Other Writings of Henry David Thoreau,* edited by Brooks Atkinson.

The great Journals themselves, about to be brought back into print; but large libraries have the earlier editions.

Henry Seidel Canby's *Thoreau* is still the most complete life (Houghton Mifflin Co., 1939).

Index

Alcott, Ames Bronson, 96, 139
Alcott, Louisa, 178 ff
Allen, Phineas, 16, 17, 34, 45
Assabet River, 27, 53

Baker Farm, 170
Bartlett, Dr. Josiah, 116
Blake, Harrison G. O., 112, 188
Brisbane, Albert, 126
Brown, John, 185 ff
Brown, Mrs. Lucy Jackson, 66, 67, 93, 107
Brownson, Orestes A., 49, 50, 52, 62, 94
Bulkeley, Peter, 9

Canada, 180 ff
Canby, Henry S., 186
Cape Cod, 181 ff
Channing, Prof. Edward Tyrell, 46, 47, 57
Channing, William Ellery, 95, 111, 136, 162, 171, 180
Civil Disobedience, 157
Collins, James, 142
Concord Academy, 9, 45
Concord Bridge, 26, 66, 78

Concord Lyceum, 33, 34, 130
Concord, Massachusetts, 25, 26 ff
Concord River, 27 ff, 145, 149, 173 ff

Dana, Richard Henry, Jr., 45
Dial, The, 118, 131, 133
Dunbar, Charles, 2 ff, 14

Emerson, Edward, 33, 69
Emerson, Haven, 123
Emerson, Lidian Jackson (Mrs. R.W.E.), 96 ff, 135 ff
Emerson, Mary Moody, 37, 114 ff
Emerson, Ralph Waldo, 17, 30, 41, 52, 53 ff, 63, 93 ff, 106 ff, 126, 138, 193
Emerson, Waldo, 117 ff
Emerson, William, 121 ff

Fair Haven, 27, 42, 133
Fitchburg Railroad, 139
Flint Pond, 137
Friendship, Essay on, 149
Fugitive Slave Law, 177

INDEX

Fuller, Margaret, 96, 113 ff

Goodwin, John (One-Eyed), 10
   ff, 15
Greeley, Horace, 126, 131

Harvard College, 16, 17, 44 ff
Harvard Library, 45 ff
Holmes, Oliver Wendell, 72
Hosmer, Horace, 102
Hosmer, Perch, 12
Hosmer, Sam, 159
Huguenots, The, 2, 3

James, Henry (senior), 123
Journal, Thoreau's, 57, 58, 75,
   92, 110, 128, 129, 147

Katadhin, Mount, 160

Lexington, 80
Life Without Principle, 177, 185
Lowell, James Russell, 45

Manse, The Old, 26
Maine, 159 ff
Maine Woods, The, 161
Melvin, George, 3
Merrimack River, 84 ff, 145,
   149, 173 ff
Mill Dam, The, 26
Minnesota, 191
Minott, George, 11, 13, 19 ff, 24
Monadnock, 27
Mott, Lucretia, 127
Musketaquid, 27

Nature, Emerson's, 52 ff
New York, 124 ff

Parker, Theodore, 45
Parkman House, 67, 129
Plea for Captain John Brown, A,
   186

Quebec, 181

Ricketson, Daniel, 188
Ripley, Dr. Ezra, 7, 15, 30, 43,
   62

Sanborn, Franklin B., 183
Sewall, Edmund, 75 ff
Sewall, Ellen, 77 ff
Sic Vita, 107, 193
Sleepy Hollow Cemetery, 193
Staples, Sam, 129, 134, 156 ff,
   192
Staten Island, 122 ff
Sudbury River, 27
Sympathy, 76

Teale, Edwin Way, 165, 199
Texas House, 130, 131, 134,
   139
Thoreau, Cynthia, 14, 16, 18,
   28, 59 ff, 74
Thoreau, Helen, 13, 14, 29, 34,
   59, 60, 94
Thoreau, Henry David
   appearance, 44, 48, 140
   ancestry, 3
   the Burns case, 184 ff
   chases a fox, 120 ff
   childhood traits, 16, 33
   clear-sightedness, 10 ff, 29, 31
   company at Walden Pond, 146

Thoreau, Henry David (*Contd.*)
  described by Edward Emerson,
    108
  dislike of parties, 36
  discovers Emerson's *Nature*,
    52 ff
  enjoyment of weather, 28
  excursion to Canada, 180 ff
  excursion to Cape Cod, 181 ff
  falls in love, 99 ff
  friends at Harvard, 45
  goes to Walden Pond, 139
  the grasshopper trick on So-
    phia, 51
  his haunts in Concord, 25, 41
  home-life, 13 ff, 29 ff
  homesickness at Cambridge,
    44
  in jail, 156 ff
  in New York, 122 ff
  interest in Indians, 7 ff, 29,
    38, 72
  joy in freedom, 7, 28
  learns through Orestes Brown-
    son, 49 ff
  love of argument, 32 ff
  love of birds, 1, 8, 12, 15, 21,
    24, 31, 154
  love of wilderness, 25 ff
  mannerisms, 60, 110
  Marco Polo, the pig, 35 ff
  Min, his cat, 12, 18, 24, 32
  on walking, 148 ff, 195 ff
  philosophizes, 8, 28, 29, 34,
    35, 37, 46, 47, 54, 55, 57,
    64, 86, 96, 99, 102, 103,
    104, 119, 125, 144, 162,
    163 ff

Thoreau, Henry David (*Contd.*)
  philosophy of compensation,
    30
  plans *Kalendar*, 187
  pleasure in words, 13, 22
  pronunciation of name, 140
  pun, 18
  rebellion against Sunday blue
    laws, 2
  the river trip, 79 ff
  school discipline, 63, 68 ff
  sense of humor, 25, 26
  sets woods afire, 132 ff
  sorrow at John's death, 116 ff
  speaks on slavery, 177
  starts Journal, 57
  teaches school, 62, 67 ff
  teaching at Canton, Massachu-
    setts, 49
  various homes, 5
  views of freedom, 8, 61, 92,
    105
  views of friendship, 91, 149 ff
  views of nature, 52, 81
  views on civilization, 31
  views on girls, 36, 50
Thoreau, Jane, 7, 14, 18
Thoreau, John (father of
    H.D.T.), 6, 16 ff, 29, 60,
    65, 75, 122, 134
Thoreau, John (brother of
    H.D.T.), 4, 8, 14 ff, 24,
    25, 40, 43 ff, 50, 65, 67,
    77 ff, 99, 101, 104 ff, 111,
    115 ff
Thoreau, Louisa, 32, 60, 64, 65
Thoreau, Maria, 3, 14 ff, 18,
    103, 174

INDEX

Thoreau, Mme. Philippe, 3

Thoreau, Sophia, 4 ff, 13 ff, 17, 31, 36 ff, 51, 59, 60, 69

Transcendentalism, 96

Wachusett, 27, 42

Walden (the book), 152, 154 ff, 165 ff, 176, 199

Walden Pond, 99, 137 ff

Ward, Prudence, 74, 99, 139 ff

Week on the Concord and Merrimack Rivers, A, 145, 149, 173 ff

Weiss, John, 48

Wheeler, Stearns, 45, 137

Whitman, Walt, 188

Willard, Simon, 4

Winter Walk, A, 190

Yankee in Canada, A, 181

T. MORRIS LONGSTRETH

was born in Philadelphia in 1886 but came more thoroughly to life when he entered Westtown Boarding School in 1899. There he passionately loved the open Pennsylvania country, made some stout friendships which last to this day, and met Henry Thoreau in the Journals. After Haverford College, he tutored in England, than taught school in Philadelphia, and liked it. But he wrote *Reading the Weather* and *The Adirondacks* at night. The latter travel book got him an invitation to live at Lake Placid Club, where he found the joys of real winter. Life in Canada followed logically, and, after studying the archives of the Royal Canadian Mounted Police and traveling with them wherever the history had been made, he wrote *The Silent Force,* their history.

In 1935, Morris Longstreth touched home base again, living five years in Washington, D. C., and seven in Concord, Massachusetts, where he frequented Thoreau's haunts and learned of his habits. Finally, he returned to Westtown, where he sees a good deal of the boys and girls who, he feels, are the real Fountain of Life, whatever Ponce de León may say.

Life, says Mr. Longstreth, has been good to him in health and habitats, in travels as far away as British Columbia, the Arctic, Moscow, and Colombia. Better still, life has presented him with marvelous friends of both sexes, as well as unseen fans who write him fascinating letters. Life has offered him its riches of reading, painting, music, sculpture, and architecture, although he is not yet a millionaire. He proposes that it go on for quite a while.